We all love the ocean's surface with its beautiful sparkle blue. But beneath it, down deeper, whales are moving with slow, drifting currents—whales that are great, gentle, cloudlike beings.

Roger Payne, whale biologist, 1991

Whales in the Classroom

Presents

Getting to Know the Whales

By Larry Wade

Drawings by
Stephen Bolles

Singing Rock Press
Minnetonka, Minnesota
1995

Whales in the Classroom
Presents
Getting to Know the Whales

By Larry Wade

Published by: Singing Rock Press
P.O. Box 1274
Minnetonka, MN 55345
Phone: (612) 935-4910

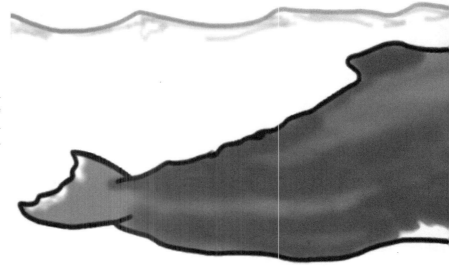

Copyright © 1995 by Lawrence S. Wade
        First Printing: April 1995
        Second Printing June 1996
Library of Congress Cataloging in Publication Data
Wade, Lawrence S. 1948-
        Getting to Know the Whales
        (Whales in the Classroom Presents)
1. Whales 2. Whales-Juvenile Literature
I. Title   II. Series

QL737.C4.W119   599.5
ISBN 0-9629395-2-8

What is *Whales in the Classroom?*

Whales in the Classroom Presents: Getting to Know the Whales is the second in a series of ocean books. The first book *Whales in the Classroom Presents: Oceanography* is about marine geology, ocean currents, plankton, and marine ecology.

This book is for middle-school-aged students who are interested in whales. It is for those who are exploring the subject for the first time and for those who are seriously considering studying whales as a career. Most of the activities presented in the book were developed from actual scientific data contributed by whale biologists. There are several interviews with whale biologists who answer questions that young scientists will want to know.

Students have played a major role in the development of *Whales in the Classroom.* Hundreds of students and teachers have used this book, and have added valuable editing comments.

This book is designed primarily for student use. However, we have included a teacher's section with answers to activities.

Important terms are *italicized* in the text, and are defined under "Terms for the Whale Biologist" on the second or third page of every chapter. Included in most chapters is an interview with a scientist, "Up Close and Personal with a Whale Biologist."

Striped Dolphin photo by James Cotton

Writer's Dedication

To the Guardians of the Earth, young and old. Those who love the Earth: swamp walkers, whale watchers, tidepoolers, tree people, froggers, backpackers, birders, and snorkellers. You are the hope for our Earth. Your voice and heart are needed to help others learn about the Earth's deep magic. Always keep the Earth in your heart. Let it nurture you and give you strength.

Artist's Dedication

Time is getting short, and the Artist in each of us must be supported. The Art in every Child is a natural part, although quite shy in many. Encourage it, resolve to not criticize it, and nurture its expression as part of Hope for the world.
Thanks, Julie, for not minding my early mornings...

Acknowledgments

I would like to thank G.V. Morejohn, formerly of Moss Landing Marine Lab, Moss Landing, CA, for inspiring my interests in whales.

Holly Einess of Edina, MN, did the meticulous work of editing the book. Sharon Votel, St. Mary's College, took precious time to review several drafts of the book. Pat Ricci contributed the Cataloging in Publication data. Hundreds of teachers and students have used the book and have contributed many ideas.

Over the past years I have received great support from a number of people and school districts: Jane Holmberg, Intermediate District 287; John Erickson, Hopkins School District 270; Priscilla Herbison, St. Mary's College; Continuing Studies classes, Hamline University; Gary Friedrichsen, Arcata, CA; James Cotton, Trinidad, CA; Paul Kelly, Cal Fish and Game; Ed Mitchell, Fisheries Research Board of Canada; and Donna Taylor, Minnetonka, MN.

Also, I would like to thank all of the marine scientists who participated in "Up Close and Personal with a Famous Whale Biologist," including: Steve Katona, Richard Sears, Roger Payne, Ken Balcomb, Bruce Mate, Carole Carlson, Amy Knowlton, and Moira Brown. I would especially like to thank Erich Hoyt for his commitment to this book. Dan O'Dell contributed an excellent article on orcas kept in captivity. Larry Foster contributed the activity on "Whale Shapes and Sizes Compared." Steve Leatherwood has contributed to both Whales in the Classroom books. His article on "Dolphins in the Jungle" appears in this volume. Data for many of the activities were supplied by Allied Whale, College of the Atlantic; Gulf Project, Fisheries Research Board of Canada; and Edward Mitchell and Howard Braham, NMFS. Photographs were contributed by many people, including Flip Nicklin, Margo Pfeiff, Vicki Rountree, Barbara Solberg, the Center for Coastal Studies, and James Cotton.

X

Whales in the Classroom

Presents

Getting to Know the Whales

Table of Contents

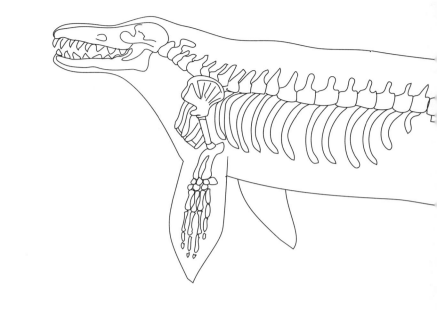

From Ocean to Land and Back

The whale is the most specialized of all mammals on Earth. It is completely adapted to life in the water. Its body is streamlined and it has no hind limbs. The whale's tail flukes are used for swimming and are not made of bone, but of a softer substance known as cartilage (your nose is made of cartilage). The whale's front limbs have evolved into flippers which are used for steering. To maintain their warm body temperature in the often frigid water and to insulate them from the cold, whales have a layer of fat, called blubber, up to 20 inches thick.

Whales still have some similarities to land mammals. They have to come to the surface to breathe air. Their young are born alive after being carried by the mother for 12-18 months. The young whale (called a calf) suckles milk from the mother's mammary glands, which are located inside her body.

There are two groups of whales. One group is known as odontoceti (o-dont-o-seat-ee), which means toothed whale, and includes the familiar bottlenose dolphin and orca. The other group is known as mystoceti (mist-o-seat-ee) or baleen (bay-leen) whales. Instead of teeth, this group of whales has fringed strainers hanging from their upper jaw. These strainers are called baleen. The baleen is used for catching and filtering out schools of fish and plankton from the water. Included in this group are blue and humpback whales. A baleen whale may have up to 400 baleen plates on each side of its upper jaw. The baleen is not a modified tooth; in fact it feels more like a fingernail.

Whales were not always found in the ocean. The story of their

Mesonychid

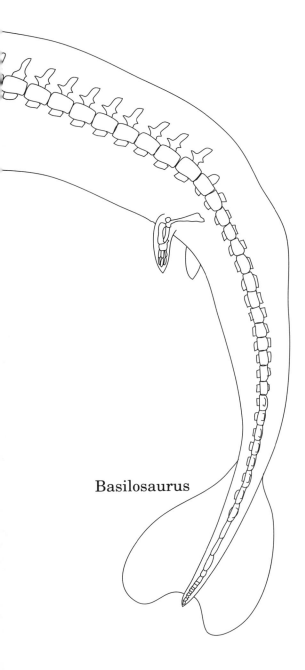

Basilosaurus

development began a long time ago. It's rather strange that while all life on Earth started microscopically in the oceans and got progressively bigger, whales—the largest of all animals—developed through evolution from land mammals and only then entered the sea. Scientists have learned about the ancestors of whales by studying fossils that were found at the edge of ancient shallow seas. The earliest known ancestors of whales, mesonychids (mez-on-i-kids), probably lived 50 million years ago at the edge of shallow bays. Mesonychids looked more like wolves but were closely related to today's ungulates (the deer family).

The adaptations that whales had to make from a life on land to a life in the seas did not occur overnight. The early whales were probably more like otters and still had a strong connection to land. It took millions of years for whales to develop fins from feet and a tail fluke for locomotion.

About 40 million years ago there was a very successful group of early whales that inhabited shallow seas. These animals were called archiocetes (ark-e-o-seat, meaning *ancient whale*), and their fossil remains have been found in ancient shallow seabeds all over the world. They ranged in size from 6 to 60 feet (2 to 20 meters). The Basilosaurus (Baa-sil-o-soar-us) was an archiocete, but was misnamed by early paleontologists (pay-lee-on-tol-o-gist, or *fossil scientist*) who thought that the mammal was a marine dinosaur. The Basilosaurus was snakelike in appearance and grew up to 50 feet long. The nostrils were positioned slightly higher on the head than on a typical land mammal, but not on top of the head like a present-day whale. In 1989, it was discovered that one species of Basilosaurus had hind legs. The legs, which had three toes, were more than 20 inches long. The parts of the legs were all there, but the animal could not use them to walk on land.

The archiocetes eventually died out 30 million years ago. By this time descendents of both present-day whale groups, toothed whales and baleen whales, were dominant in the seas. The early baleen whales were called cetotheres (see-toe-theers). Early cetotheres still had teeth, but the teeth were adapted for straining water, like the baleen of present-day whales. The early toothed whales were called squaladonts (skwa-la-donts). Many of the squaladonts looked like present-day orca whales and probably had a similar diet.

How to Draw a Whale

The Old Whale Biologist

Many people are afraid to draw. Years ago, when I had my first big job studying whales, the principal investigator of the study looked at me and told me that all of my field notes had to be illustrated. My jaw dropped...and I looked blankly at him. I had not drawn anything in 22 years! I spent the next two months struggling with my whale drawings. Well, within four months I was an expert whale illustrator! My field notes were much more detailed and I was a better observer because I had to look for the details in order to draw my subjects. Drawing is another way of seeing and describing. All people can draw; however, some are more gifted than others. Practice will definitely help the illustrator to improve his or her skills. The biologist who draws has another tool which she or he can use out in the field.

What We Will Discover

In this section we will discover the joys of drawing and illustrating. In making our drawing of a whale, we will discover some of the adaptations of whales to their environment.

How We Will Do This

We will follow the step-by-step process described for drawing a whale. We will label the parts of a whale on our finished drawing.

Terms for the Whale Biologist

The Whale's Body Parts

Blowhole - The *blowhole* is the nose of the whale. It is located behind the bump (*splash guard*) on the top of the whale's head. The splash guard protects the whale from getting water into its blowhole.

Dorsal Fin - *Dorsal* means "topside." The dorsal fin is believed to act as a keel to keep the whale oriented upright. The male killer whale has a dorsal fin six feet high. However, some whales (the gray and humpback) have no dorsal fin at all.

Ear - The *ear* opening is a tiny, nonfunctional hole located behind and slightly above the eye. Sound is one of the main ways that whales perceive their environment. They communicate with each other and use sound to navigate. The sound vibrations travel through the whale's body to its inner ear and are not received through the ear opening.

Eye - The *eyes* are located on each side of body, near the end of the mouth. The whale can only see to the side, not directly in front of itself. Since visibility in the ocean is so limited, sight is not an important sense.

Flipper - The *flipper* is equivalent to the human hand and arm and is used for turning. Humpback whales have large *flippers* which they use for locomotion.

Flukes - The tail *flukes* are lobes on a whale's tail and are the primary structure used for swimming. The flukes move up and down (*vertically*). Most fish move their tails sideways (*horizontally*).

Mammary Glands - *Mammary glands* are milk-producing organs situated inside the female whale's body. (This location maintains the streamlined shape of the whale.) The glands are located on the ventral side (*underside*) of the whale, close to the tail. If a young calf wants to nurse, the mother turns slightly on its side. The young calf bumps the mammary gland with its mouth, and the milk is ejected. A blue whale calf may gain close to 200 pounds a day, just drinking its mother's milk.

Rostrum - The *rostrum* is the long flat ridge on the dorsal side of a baleen whale's head, extending from the blowhole to the tip of the mouth.

Ventral Pleats - The *ventral pleats* are grooves on the underside of a whale's mouth that expand when feeding so the mouth can hold more water.

Now, let's draw a whale!

First, draw the rostrum...

Next, draw the belly of the whale...

Next, draw the dorsal fin and the top of the whale...

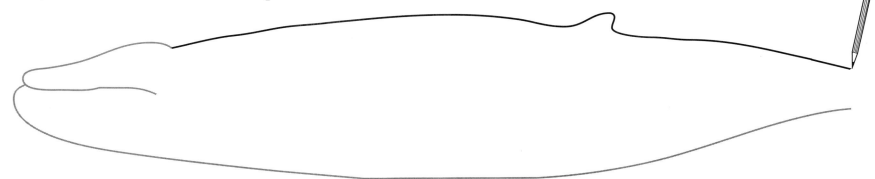

Then, add the tail flukes...

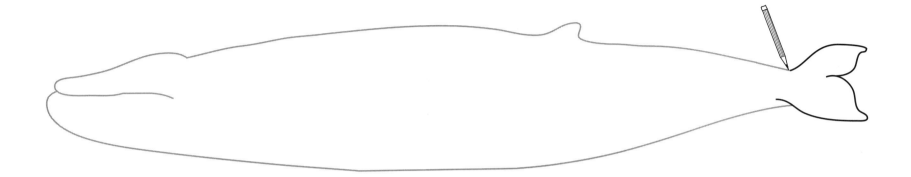

And finally, add the flipper, eye, and ventral pleats to complete your whale!

So You Want to Be a Whale Biologist

Now, draw your own whale on this page.

After drawing your own whale, label the parts of the whale below. At the bottom of the page are listed each of the parts you must find.

If you need help with names of the whale parts, check "Terms for the Whale Biologist" on pages 4 and 5.

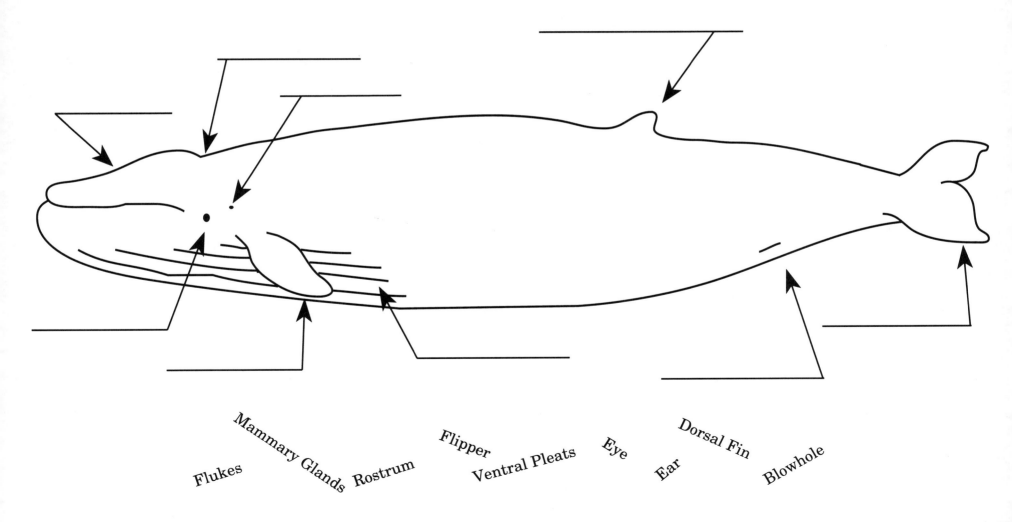

Flukes   Mammary Glands   Rostrum   Flipper   Ventral Pleats   Eye   Ear   Dorsal Fin   Blowhole

Getting to Know the Whales

The Old Whale Biologist

One of the first jobs I had as a whale biologist was on the St. Lawrence River in Quebec, Canada. I drove across the country in a beat-up car to work on the project. I had just finished a yearlong study on sea otters and I felt like I was on my way up in the scientific world. The truth is I knew nothing about whales. In fact, it took me a week to figure out the difference between a minke whale and a fin whale. (Trust me! Minkes are really different from fin whales.) But I was totally into whales. I would work 16 hours a day and think nothing of it. I was so immersed in whales, they started visiting me in my dreams. I'll never forget a dream I had about a fin whale that swam up to me and turned its head and looked me directly in the eye. I can still see that eye staring at me.

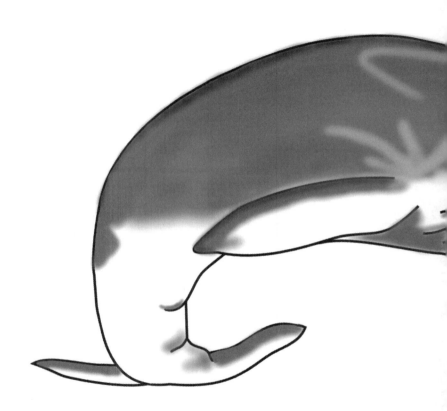

The chief scientist of the project told me that blue whales inhabited the St. Lawrence River. To me, the blue whale was a living dinosaur, a giant lost in the mists of time. As far as I knew the blue whale was on the verge of extinction due to extensive whaling. I can clearly remember the first blue whale I ever saw. I was sitting on top of our trailer at our research camp and looking out on the water. I saw some tall whale spouts downriver, but could not tell what type of whale was producing the spouts. Twelve minutes later, the whale surfaced again right in front of us. There were three of us on the trailer and we knew immediately what it was. We were speechless at first, then someone whispered, "It's a blue!" I was supposed to be a professional scientist, but I found myself jumping up and down and screaming with joy. Who says that scientists are cold, objective, and passionless?

Then there were the sightings of the "mystery whale." It was 20 to 30 feet long, brown in color, and had a hooked dorsal fin. I saw the whale three different times and each time I had a feeling in my gut that the whale was something rare and unknown to science. It was an exciting feeling, seeing something that other humans knew nothing about. I am sure it was some kind of rare beaked whale. It

has been more than 25 years since I sighted that whale and I still wonder what *species* it was.

What We Will Discover

In this section we will discover how biologists *classify* whales and will develop skills in observing species characteristics. We also will discover how to use a *key* , and get to know the characteristics of many different groups of whales.

How We Will Do This

We will be given drawings of various whales and dolphins. Our job will be to identify the whale by using a whale and dolphin key. After the whale is identified, it can be placed on a whale family tree.

Terms for the Whale Biologist

Classify - To *classify* is to make an effort to arrange animals or plants into related groups. Individuals with similar characteristics are classified into similar groups.

Key - A *key* is a scientific tool used to identify individual animals and plants based upon their physical characteristics. The user of a key will make a series of choices about the life-form in question in an attempt to identify it.

Scale - *Scale* is a measured length used to represent a larger unit of measure (e.g. one inch = six feet).

Species - A *species* is a distinct type of animal or plant.

How to Use the Whale and Dolphin Key

Choose one of the whales on pages 14 and 15. In this example, we will use the whale marked **"L"** on page 15.

1. Measure the total length of the whale in inches.

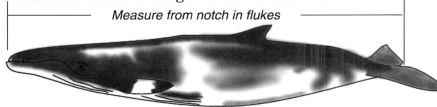

Measure from notch in flukes

This whale is about 4 inches in length.

2. Read the scale under whale "L": for this whale it says 1 inch = 6.6 ft.

3. Multiply the length you measured by the scale:

4 inches x 6.6 feet = 26.4 feet

Record the total length beneath the picture of the whale.

Next, go to the Whale and Dolphin Key on pages 16 and 17. To find out what species whale "L" is, you must go through the key, looking for characteristics of your whale. Then, go back to the whale drawings on page 15 and write in your whale's name. You will follow this procedure for each of the 14 whales on pages 14 and 15. But first, follow the directions for using the key and identify whale "L."

Using the Key

1. If you can't remember what some of the physical characteristics of whales are, it might be good to review the activity "How to Draw a Whale," at the beginning of this chapter.

2. Start at the beginning of the key. For the whale above, decide if a rostrum is present or absent. Since this whale has a rostrum, we follow the arrow down.

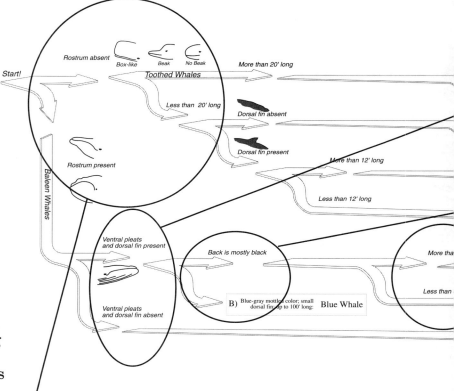

3. Next we must choose whether the ventral pleats and dorsal fin are present or absent. Since the pleats and fin are present, we follow the arrow at the top.

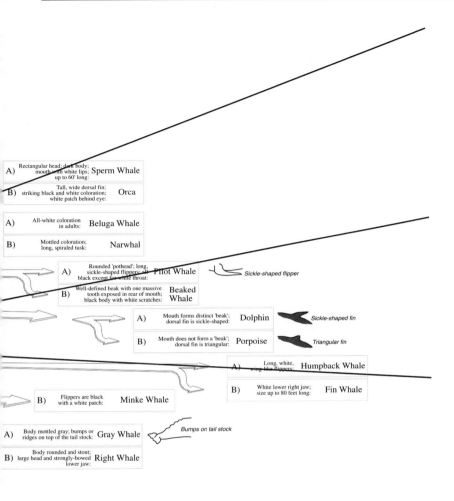

A) Rectangular head; dark body; mouth with white lips; up to 60' long: **Sperm Whale**

B) Tall, wide dorsal fin; striking black and white coloration; white patch behind eye: **Orca**

A) All-white coloration in adults: **Beluga Whale**

B) Mottled coloration; long, spiraled tusk: **Narwhal**

A) Rounded 'pothead'; long, sickle-shaped flippers; all black except for white throat: **Pilot Whale**
Sickle-shaped flipper

B) Well-defined beak with one massive tooth exposed in rear of mouth; black body with white scratches: **Beaked Whale**

A) Mouth forms distinct 'beak'; dorsal fin is sickle-shaped: **Dolphin**
Sickle-shaped fin

B) Mouth does not form a 'beak'; dorsal fin is triangular: **Porpoise**
Triangular fin

A) Long, white, wing-like flippers: **Humpback Whale**

B) White lower right jaw; size up to 80 feet long: **Fin Whale**

B) Flippers are black with a white patch: **Minke Whale**

A) Body mottled gray; bumps or ridges on top of the tail stock: **Gray Whale**
Bumps on tail stock

B) Body rounded and stout; large head and strongly-bowed lower jaw: **Right Whale**

4. The next choice is whether the whale's back is mostly black or a blue-gray, mottled color. This whale's back is mostly black. Follow the arrow at the top.

5. Last, we must decide whether the whale's body length is more than 30 feet or less than 30 feet. Initially we calculated a length of 26 feet, which makes it a minke whale! Write the name of whale "L" beneath the picture.

Now, go through the Whale and Dolphin Key on pages 16 and 17 to complete this process for each of the other 13 whales on pages 14 and 15.

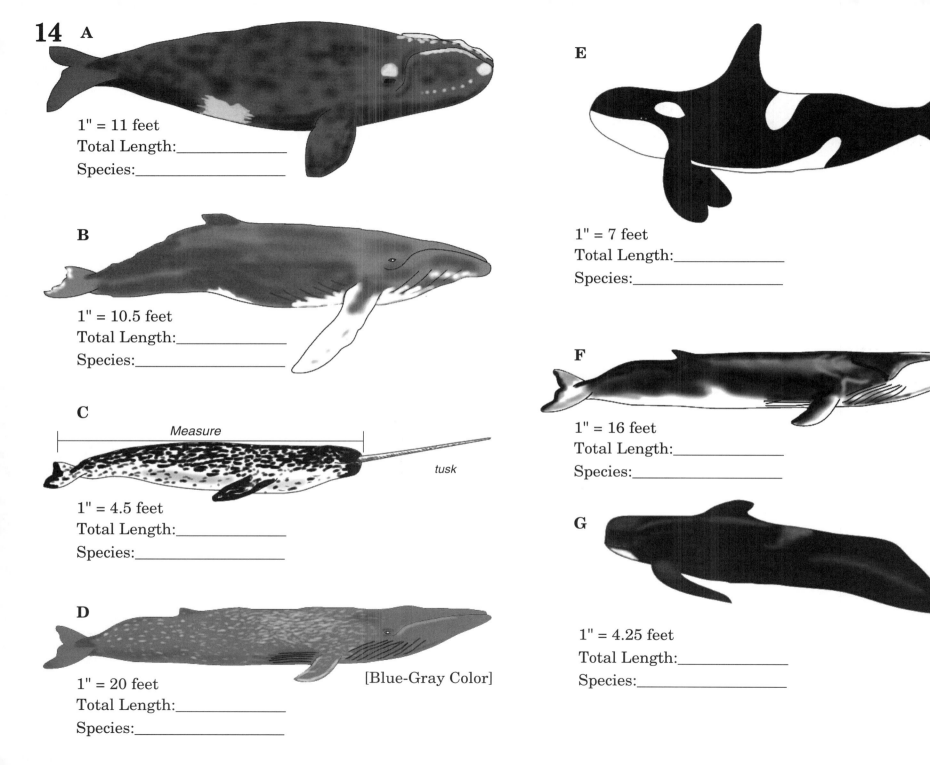

14 **A**

1" = 11 feet

Total Length:_____

Species:_____

B

1" = 10.5 feet

Total Length:_____

Species:_____

C

Measure

tusk

1" = 4.5 feet

Total Length:_____

Species:_____

D

1" = 20 feet

[Blue-Gray Color]

Total Length:_____

Species:_____

E

1" = 7 feet

Total Length:_____

Species:_____

F

1" = 16 feet

Total Length:_____

Species:_____

G

1" = 4.25 feet

Total Length:_____

Species:_____

H *tooth*

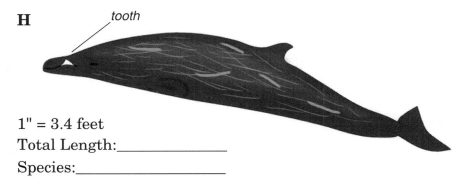

1" = 3.4 feet

Total Length:_____

Species:_____

K

1" = 1.6 feet

Total Length:_____

Species:_____

I

1" = 10.3 feet

Total Length:_____

Species:_____

L

1" = 6.6 feet

Total Length:_____

Species:_____

M

1" = 12 feet

Total Length:_____

Species:_____

J

1" = 1.5 feet

Total Length:_____

Species:_____

N

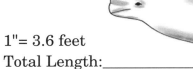

1"= 3.6 feet

Total Length:_____

Species:_____

Whale and

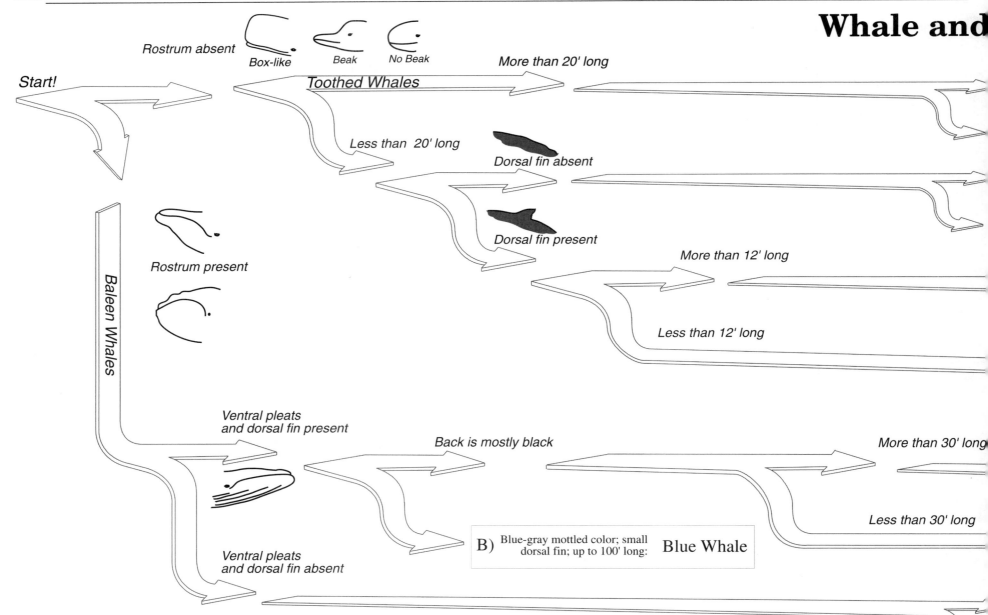

Start!

Rostrum absent

Box-like

Beak

No Beak

Toothed Whales

More than 20' long

Less than 20' long

Dorsal fin absent

Dorsal fin present

Baleen Whales

Rostrum present

More than 12' long

Less than 12' long

Ventral pleats and dorsal fin present

Back is mostly black

More than 30' long

B) Blue-gray mottled color; small dorsal fin; up to 100' long: **Blue Whale**

Less than 30' long

Ventral pleats and dorsal fin absent

Dolphin Key

A) Rectangular head; dark body; mouth with white lips; up to 60' long: Sperm Whale

B) Tall, wide dorsal fin; striking black and white coloration; white patch behind eye: Orca

A) All-white coloration in adults: Beluga Whale

B) Mottled coloration; long, spiraled tusk: Narwhal

A) Rounded 'pothead'; long, sickle-shaped flippers; all black except for white throat: Pilot Whale

Sickle-shaped flipper

B) Well-defined beak with one massive tooth exposed in rear of mouth; black body with white scratches: Beaked Whale

A) Mouth forms distinct 'beak'; dorsal fin is sickle-shaped: Dolphin

Sickle-shaped fin

B) Mouth does not form a 'beak'; dorsal fin is triangular: Porpoise

Triangular fin

A) Long, white, wing-like flippers: Humpback Whale

B) White lower right jaw; size up to 80 feet long: Fin Whale

B) Flippers are black with a white patch: Minke Whale

A) Body mottled gray; bumps or ridges on top of the tail stock: Gray Whale

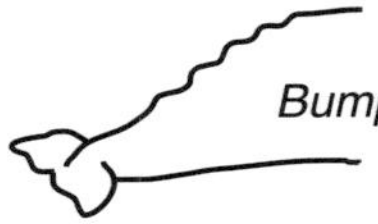

Bumps on tail stock

B) Body rounded and stout; large head and strongly-bowed lower jaw: Right Whale

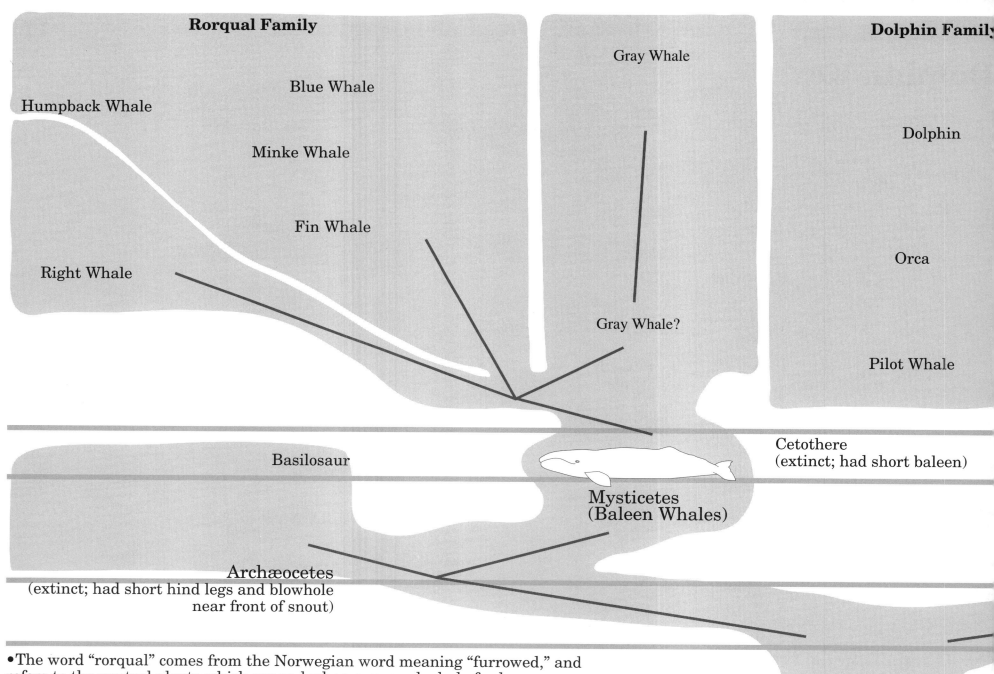

Rorqual Family

Gray Whale

Blue Whale

Humpback Whale

Minke Whale

Dolphin Family

Dolphin

Fin Whale

Right Whale

Orca

Gray Whale?

Pilot Whale

Cetothere
(extinct; had short baleen)

Basilosaur

Mysticetes
(Baleen Whales)

Archæocetes
(extinct; had short hind legs and blowhole
near front of snout)

• The word "rorqual" comes from the Norwegian word meaning "furrowed," and refers to the ventral pleats which expand when a rorqual whale feeds.
• The word "monodont" means "one-toothed."
• The gray whale is placed twice on the Family Tree because scientists disagree about when it evolved.

Mesonychid

Whale Family Tree Cutout Page

So You Want to be a Whale Biologist

The **Whale Family Tree** shows the relationships between whales and dolphins. After you have filled out the **Whale Identification Key** on pages 14 and 15, cut out the animals on this page and paste them where they belong on the tree.

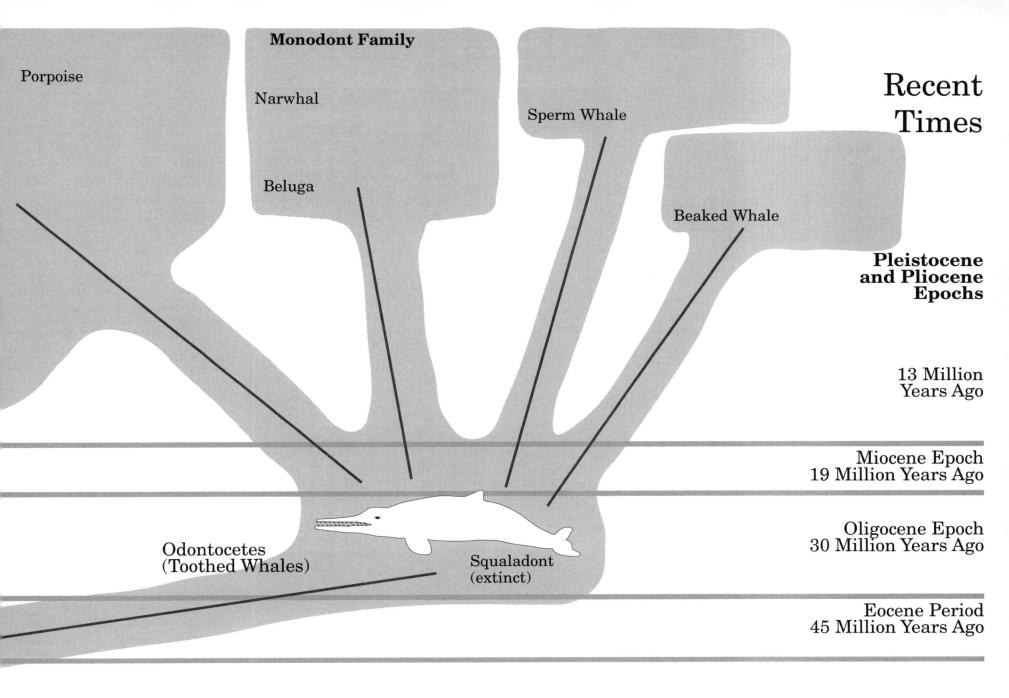

Porpoise

Monodont Family

Narwhal

Beluga

Sperm Whale

Beaked Whale

Recent Times

Pleistocene and Pliocene Epochs

13 Million Years Ago

Miocene Epoch 19 Million Years Ago

Oligocene Epoch 30 Million Years Ago

Odontocetes (Toothed Whales)

Squaladont (extinct)

Eocene Period 45 Million Years Ago

Paleocene Epoch 60 Million Years Ago

The Whale Family Tree

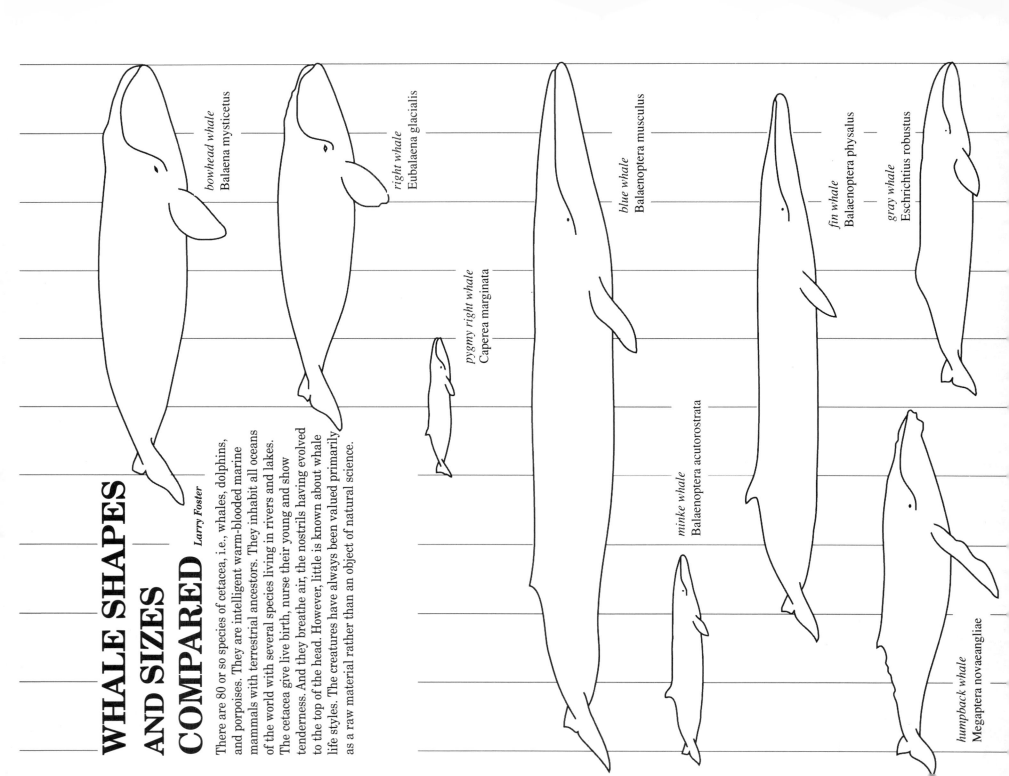

WHALE SHAPES AND SIZES COMPARED

Larry Foster

There are 80 or so species of cetacea, i.e., whales, dolphins, and porpoises. They are intelligent warm-blooded marine mammals with terrestrial ancestors. They inhabit all oceans of the world with several species living in rivers and lakes. The cetacea give live birth, nurse their young and show tenderness. And they breathe air, the nostrils having evolved to the top of the head. However, little is known about whale life styles. The creatures have always been valued primarily as a raw material rather than an object of natural science.

bowhead whale
Balaena mysticetus

right whale
Eubalaena glacialis

pygmy right whale
Caperea marginata

blue whale
Balaenoptera musculus

minke whale
Balaenoptera acutorostrata

fin whale
Balaenoptera physalus

gray whale
Eschrichtius robustus

humpback whale
Megaptera novaeangliae

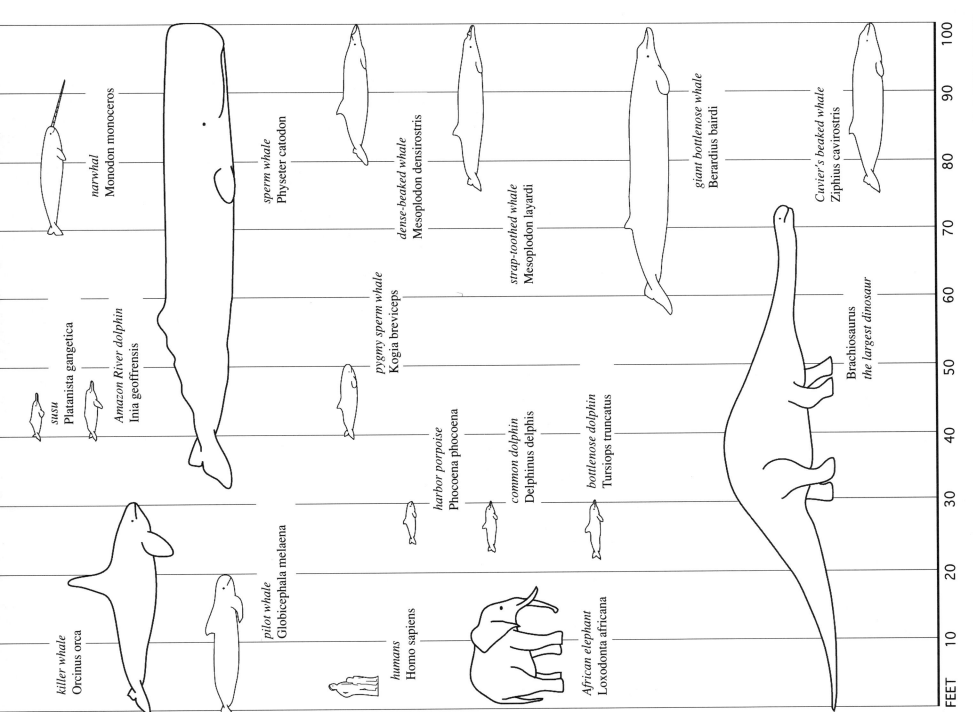

killer whale
Orcinus orca

pilot whale
Globicephala melaena

susu
Platanista gangetica

Amazon River dolphin
Inia geoffrensis

narwhal
Monodon monoceros

sperm whale
Physeter catodon

pygmy sperm whale
Kogia breviceps

dense-beaked whale
Mesoplodon densirostris

strap-toothed whale
Mesoplodon layardi

harbor porpoise
Phocoena phocoena

common dolphin
Delphinus delphis

bottlenose dolphin
Tursiops truncatus

giant bottlenose whale
Berardius bairdi

Cuvier's beaked whale
Ziphius cavirostris

humans
Homo sapiens

African elephant
Loxodonta africana

Brachiosaurus
the largest dinosaur

FEET   10   20   30   40   50   60   70   80   90   100

Artwork after Foster, with gratitude

Dolphins in the Jungle.... Impossible!

Steve Leatherwood, Cetacean Specialist Group, Solana Beach, CA, 1993.

Steve Leatherwood has been a researcher of whales and dolphins for more than 20 years. An interview with Steve appeared in <u>Whales in the Classroom Volume 1: Oceanography.</u>

Mention the word dolphin in most parts of the world and you might see images of small sea mammals leaping and cavorting in the blue depths of the ocean sea, the blue-green waters of the continental shelf, or the wave-churned waters along the seashore. This is the usual domain of the world's dolphins, the small cousins to whales. But to residents of the upper Amazon/Maranon Rivers in South America, the word dolphin paints an entirely different picture.

Unlikely as it seems, the snakelike waterways through the rich green jungle of Peru (in fact, almost all of the Amazon Basin) are home to not one, but two dolphin species. The first river dolphin, the tucuxi (or *bufeo negro*, as it is called in Peru), is a spitting image of the familiar bottlenose dolphin found in tropical and temperate marine waters all over the world. But here the similarities end. The second river dolphin, the pink boto, is directly related to three other so-called river dolphins: the susu or bhulan in the major rivers of the Indian subcontinent; the baiji, in the Yangtze River of the People's Republic of China; the franciscana, in coastal waters of eastern South America from southern Brazil to central Argentina.

The tucuxi live in small herds found mostly in the deeper channels of the main river and larger tributaries. Even when the rivers rise dramatically during the annual rains, flooding vast tracts of jungle to depths of up to 40 feet, the tucuxi continue to make their living in these channels and in the deeper lakes formed or enlarged by the flood waters. It is remarkable that they can survive in fresh water, since most dolphins are marine animals. They do confine themselves to deeper water; this is in keeping with the lifestyle of their marine relatives.

But the boto flies in the face of all convention. The calves are born all gray and look like little inflatable toys. By the time they are a

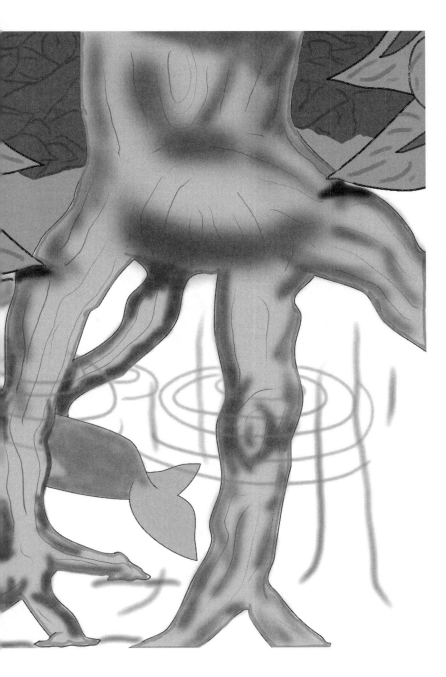

few years old, though, boto have begun to brighten to shades of gray and pink. Some even become the color of bright pink bubble gum. As if this were not enough, they have a long thick snout with whiskers all over it, a lumpy head with huge cheeks (recalling the face of a squirrel taking more nuts than it can really carry), and a long low ridge on the back that gives it a primitive alligator-like appearance. These strange beasts swim through their usually murky world without much benefit of vision; their eyes are small slits and their vision is not very good. They depend instead on a fine echolocation system (*the ability to make sounds and listen for what the echoes tell them about their surroundings*). Try closing your eyes in a small room, making noise, and listening to the echoes. Now try the same experiment outside. Imagine if that were the only way you could find your way around. That is what these dolphins do.

Like tucuxi, boto live mostly in the deep channels at the low water season. But when the flood waters invade the jungles, so do some of the boto. What a sight to watch! Pink dolphins swimming in muddy water near the treetops! Why risk entanglement in limbs and vines? Well, it seems that the flood causes many trees to drop their seeds and nuts, at a time when the river will spread them to other areas. Fish are waiting to eat some of those nuts; and dolphins are there to take the fish. This is how nature works, in a remarkable series of adaptations. And there in the midst of it all are Indians in dugout canoes, fishing among the trees. These Indians have developed legends about the dolphins that share the flooded forest with them.

It is important to know that river dolphins are being squeezed out of their natural habitat by humans. The baiji, a small river dolphin, is clinging tenuously to survival (there are only about 200 left) in the Yangtze River, China. Imagine the pollution in a river whose banks are home to nearly 12 percent of the world's population. The susu, a dolphin that lives in the Ganges River in India, is threatened by industrial pollution and heavy fishing pressure. The meat of this dolphin is relished by a local fishing caste in India. The oil of the dolphin is used as a fish attractant and for medicinal purposes. It is feared that at least one, maybe two, of the five species of river dolphins described here will be lost forever within this century.

Living the Life of a Whale

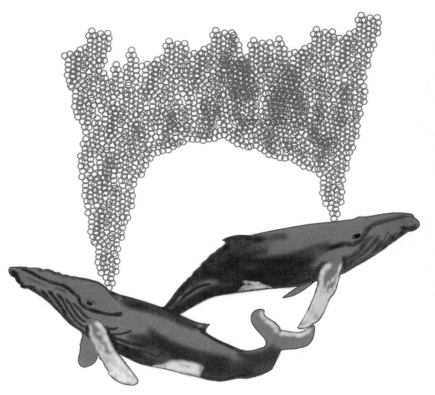

The Old Whale Biologist

Over the years, whales have shown that they are incredible ocean-ographers. They are able to locate super dense concentrations of plankton that oceanographers with expensive scientific equipment are unable to find. Also, they can find the edges of *upwellings* that are usually abundant with food.

Whales are opportunists. If there is a big school of baitfish available, then they will feed on baitfish. A few years back (1987-88), the sand lance (*a type of baitfish and an important food of the hump-backs*) were not available to the whales. But there were abundant schools of mackerel in the area. The whales feasted on them. Unfortunately, the mackerel had eaten plankton that were toxic from a natural occurrence called *red tide*. More than 14 humpbacks were found dead from the mackerel they had eaten. Being an opportunist isn't always good.

Years ago, I was on a ship out of Cape Cod, Massachusetts. There were four whales feeding together on baitfish and making what is known as *bubble clouds* beneath the surface. On one occasion the bubble cloud was emitted close to the bow of the ship where I was standing. Twenty seconds later, two of the whales surfaced in the center of the bubble cloud with their mouths wide open, water and fish streaming out of their lower jaws. I could see the dark baleen hanging down from the upper jaw. Special moments like this one have sparked my lifelong passion for studying whales.

What We Will Discover

In this chapter we will explore the feeding anatomy of whales. We also will study the feeding behavior of whales.

How We Will Do This

Initially we will track food as it moves through a whale's body. We will identify feeding strategies of different whales. We will make a flip book that shows how a baleen whale feeds.

Terms for the Whale Biologist

Behavior - The response of an animal to its environment.

Bubble Cloud - A hunting strategy used by whales. For instance, they will swim into a school of baitfish and emit a cloud of bubbles. The fish will become frightened and clump together near the surface. This makes it easier for the whale to get a mouthful of fish.

Echolocation - A process for locating objects by means of sound waves. A sound is emitted and an echo is reflected back to the emitter (for instance a dolphin) after the sound waves come in contact with an object.

Frequency - The number of sound waves produced per second.

Plankton - Floating animals (*zooplankton*) and plants (*phytoplankton*) that form the basis of food in the world's oceans.

Red Tide - The name comes from the reddish color of the seawater produced by a type of phytoplankton called dinoflagellates. Not all *red tides* are red and they have nothing to do with the tides. The red tide is sometimes triggered by excess runoff in the ocean after a heavy rain, or warmer than usual water temperatures. These conditions are favorable for bacterial growth. With an excess of bacteria in the water dinoflagellates will produce a toxin.

Upwelling - *Upwelling* is the vertical movement of water up to the ocean surface from the ocean floor. In the process, nutrients from the ocean floor are transported to the surface and can be used by phytoplankton, which are then eaten by whales. [See *Whales in the Classroom Presents: Oceanography*.]

DID ANY OTHERS ESCAPE?

A FEW MADE IT OUT OF HER MOUTH BEFORE WE WERE WIPED OFF THE BALEEN BY HER TONGUE!

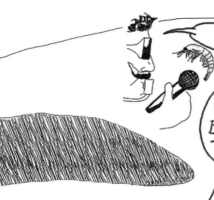

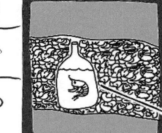

THEN WE WERE WHISKED THROUGH THE OPENING IN THE **THROAT**—ABOUT THE SIZE OF A BASKETBALL— AND TOOK A RIDE DOWN THE **ESOPHAGUS**.

THEN WE SLID INTO THIS HUMONGOUS **FORESTOMACH** CRAMMED IN THERE WITH A TON OF KRILL AND OTHER FISH. THE WALLS OF THE STOMACH BEGAN TO MASH US UP! THERE WERE EVEN SOME STONES IN THERE THAT GROUND UP MANY OF THE CRITTERS!

THEN WE WENT IN THE **MID-STOMACH**. IT WAS LIKE A SOUP IN THERE! THE ACID WAS STRONG THERE. I WATCHED FROM THE SAFETY OF MY BOTTLE AS EVERYTHING ELSE BECAME LIQUIFIED BEFORE MY EYES!

THAT'S ENOUGH! IT'S JUST BEFORE LUNCH! THEN WHAT HAPPENED?

SO HOW DID YOU GET OUT OF THE WHALE?

WELL, I HAD TO GO THROUGH THE **INTESTINES**. IN SOME WHALES THESE ARE 500 FEET LONG! IT WAS LIKE A LONG ROLLER COASTER RIDE, WITH ALL THE CURVES AND BUMPS! THE INTESTINES ARE WHERE NUTRIENTS ARE ABSORBED. ALMOST EVERYTHING GOT USED BUT MY BOTTLE, A BAG, FISH SKELETONS AND THE KRILL **EXOSKELETONS**. I CAME OUT THE **VENT** AFTER A WHOLE AFTERNOON IN THE WHALE!

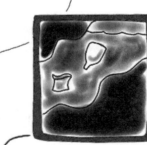

THE **PYLORIC STOMACH** WAS THE LAST OF THE THREE STOMACHS. IT HAD EVEN MORE ACID TO COMPLETE THE JOB. BY NOW, EVERYTHING WAS LIQUID EXCEPT FOR MY BOTTLE AND A PLASTIC BAG. I'VE HEARD THAT WHALES HAVE **DIED** BECAUSE PLASTIC'S GOTTEN STUCK INSIDE!

So You Want to Be a Whale Biologist

Label the diagram to the right using the information below.

Baleen - Baleen are the fringy plates that hang from the roof of a baleen whale's mouth. They are made of a material that is very similar to a person's fingernail. Their purpose is to filter the plankton and small fish from the water. The length of the baleen varies with the species of whale. The baleen of the minke whale, a fish eater, are less than six inches in length, while the baleen of a right whale get up to 12 feet long. This whale feeds on plankton living near the surface of the water.

Esophagus - The esophagus is the tube that carries the food from the mouth to the stomach. The opening on baleen whales is slightly larger than the size of a basketball on baleen whales. Although they eat large amounts of food, their prey is small and can fit through this opening. An orca—which will swallow a porpoise whole—has a much larger esophagus.

Forestomach - The forestomach is the first stomach of a baleen whale. A blue whale will fill the forestomach four times a day. The first and second stomachs will hold up to a ton of food at one time. The forestomach has a thick lining (three inches thick) and is surrounded by muscles that help to automatically grind up the food. Many toothed whales (e.g. pilot whales) have been found to have stones and pebbles in their stomachs. These are thought to aid in this grinding process.

Intestine - The intestine is important in absorbing the nutrients from the food once it is broken down by the stomachs. The intestine of a baleen whale is five to six times the length of the whale (e.g. an 80 foot blue may have intestines 400-550 feet long).

Midstomach - The midstomach is the second of the whale's three stomachs. This stomach further breaks down the food so that it can be absorbed later in the digestive process.

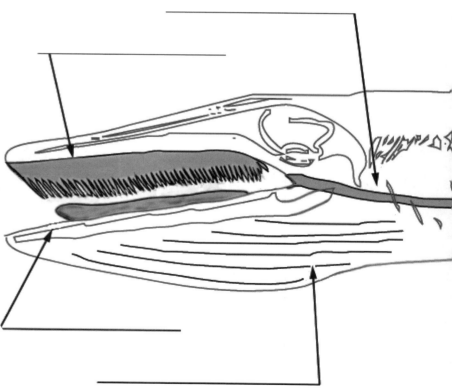

Pyloric Stomach - The pyloric stomach is the third and last stomach before the intestine. Its shape looks more like a large intestine than a stomach. Beyond the pyloric stomach is the ampulla of the large intestine (*an enlarged area of the intestine*) which has been called a fourth stomach by some scientists.

Tongue - The tongue of a blue whale is up to 20 feet long and weighs four tons (the weight of an elephant). When the whale has a mouthful of water, it pushes its tongue up to drive the water out. The food that is left on the inside of the baleen is wiped off by the tongue and swallowed.

Ventral Pleats - The ventral pleats are on the underside (ventral side) of the whale. They consist of a series of grooves that expand out when the whale takes in a mouthful of water. When the water leaves the whale's mouth the ventral pleats return to their original streamlined shape.

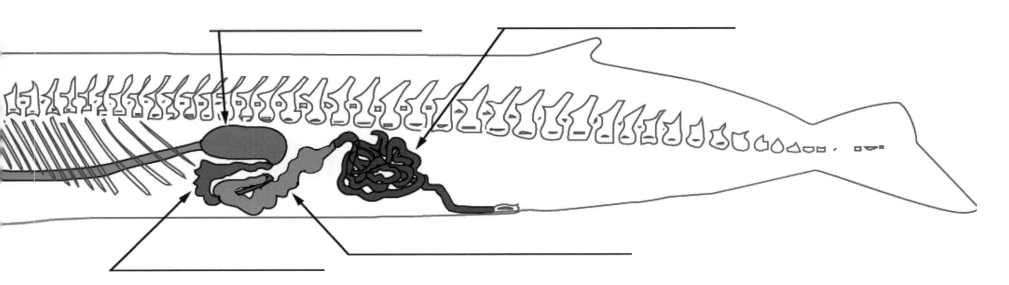

30

So You Want to Be a Whale Biologist

Below are descriptions of seven major ways in which whales feed. These techniques vary by species and also by available food supply. Read each strategy listed below and match the strategy with the picture on the following pages.

A. Suckers - Gray whales are *suckers* and **feed on the bottom** in shallow water. A gray whale pushes its tongue forward, causing water to jet out of its mouth and stir up the bottom sediments. Then as the whale draws its tongue in, this "slurry" of sediments and prey is sucked into its mouth. Often muddy water has been observed streaming out of a gray whale's mouth as it filters its prey. Gray whales feed on the bottom because their food (amphipods—pronounced "am-fi-pod"—bug-like creatures) can be abundant (10,000/ square meter).

B. Lunge Feeders - The blue and fin whales are fast moving and capable of herding a school of baitfish or krill into a tight mass and **rushing at them suddenly.** Their throats have a number of grooves or ventral pleats. The pleats expand outward and permit the whales to take in up to 15,000 gallons of water at one time (enough to fill the size of a large living room). To discharge the water from their mouths, whales contract their muscular pleats and push their tongues up.

C. Skim Feeders - When right whales are feeding they keep their mouths open continuously and **feed close to the surface** on patches of thick soupy plankton. One of their primary foods are copepods (pronounced "cope-a-pod"—quarter inch long crustaceans) which are considered to be the most numerous animals found on Earth. Right whales have extremely long baleen (up to 12 feet) which allow them to filter 20 cubic yards (the size of approximately two dump truck beds) of water per minute.

D. Bubble Cloud Feeders - A whale will **swim beneath a school of fish and release a huge cloud of bubbles**. To the fish caught in the cloud, it is like being in a blizzard. They become

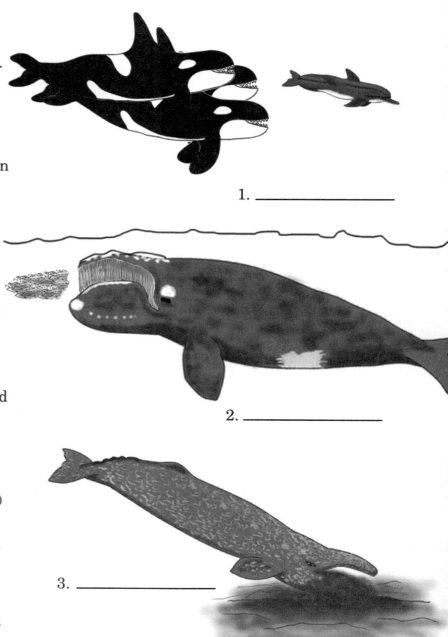

1. _____

2. _____

3. _____

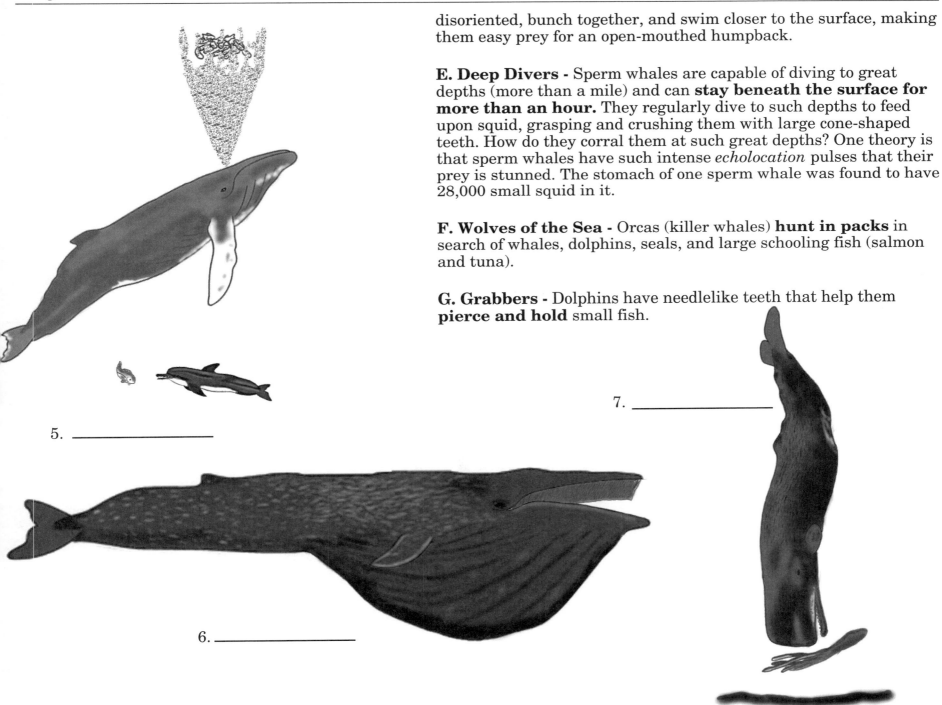

disoriented, bunch together, and swim closer to the surface, making them easy prey for an open-mouthed humpback.

E. Deep Divers - Sperm whales are capable of diving to great depths (more than a mile) and can **stay beneath the surface for more than an hour.** They regularly dive to such depths to feed upon squid, grasping and crushing them with large cone-shaped teeth. How do they corral them at such great depths? One theory is that sperm whales have such intense *echolocation* pulses that their prey is stunned. The stomach of one sperm whale was found to have 28,000 small squid in it.

F. Wolves of the Sea - Orcas (killer whales) **hunt in packs** in search of whales, dolphins, seals, and large schooling fish (salmon and tuna).

G. Grabbers - Dolphins have needlelike teeth that help them **pierce and hold** small fish.

7. _____

5. _____

6. _____

Lunge Feeding Flip-Book Activity

For this activity, you will need a pair of scissors to cut out the next three pages.

1. Cut out the next three pages along the vertical dotted lines at the left of each page. Then cut out each of the 18 panels. At the base of each panel cut along the dotted line.

2. Place the panels in order, following the numbers from 1-18.

3. The top of the panels should be flat against each other. The base of the panels should fan out, with the first panel being the smallest and the last panel being the largest.

4. Staple them all together on the dotted line in the center of the first panel.

5. Hold the book with one hand at the top, where the staple is. To see the whale lunge and eat its fill of plankton and squeeze out the tons of extra water it takes in, flip the pages with your other hand, like this:

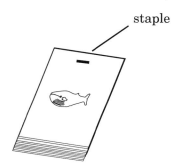

staple

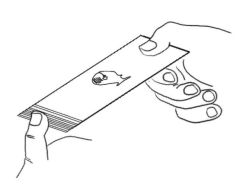

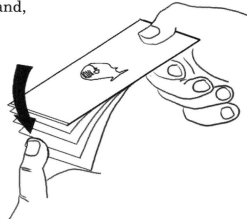

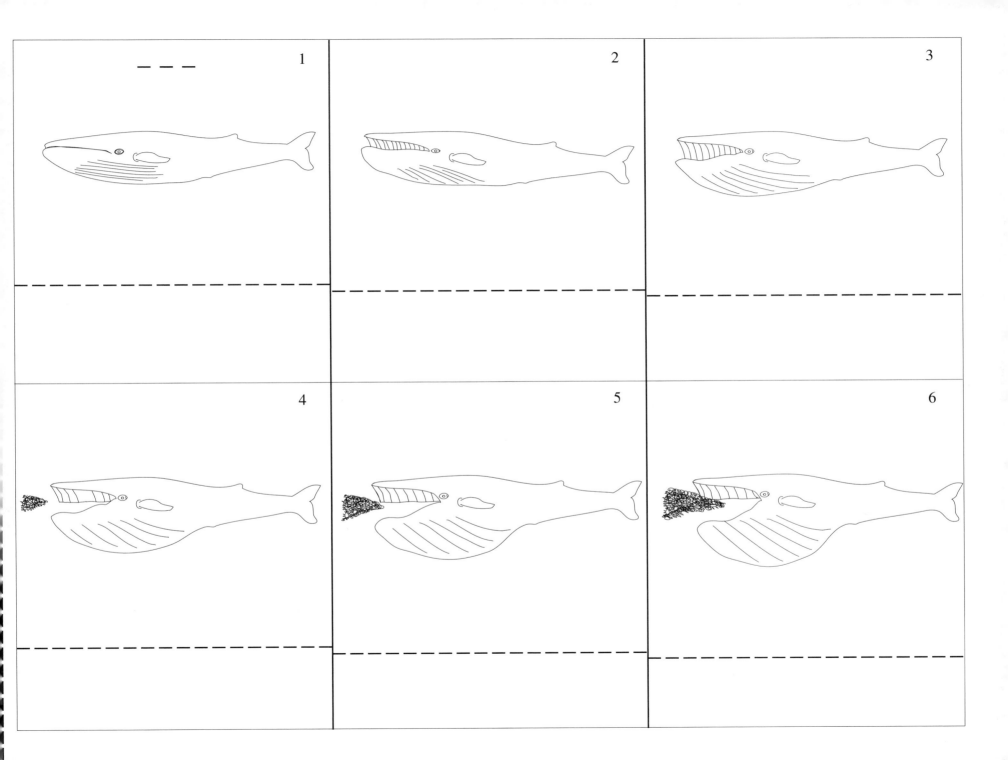

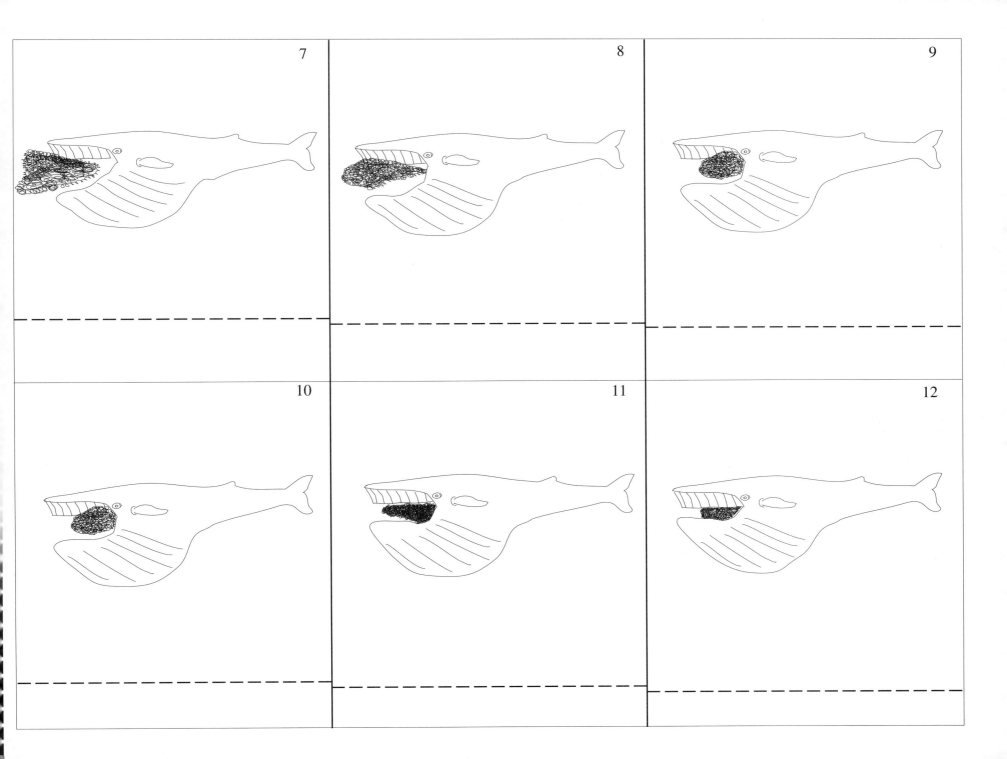

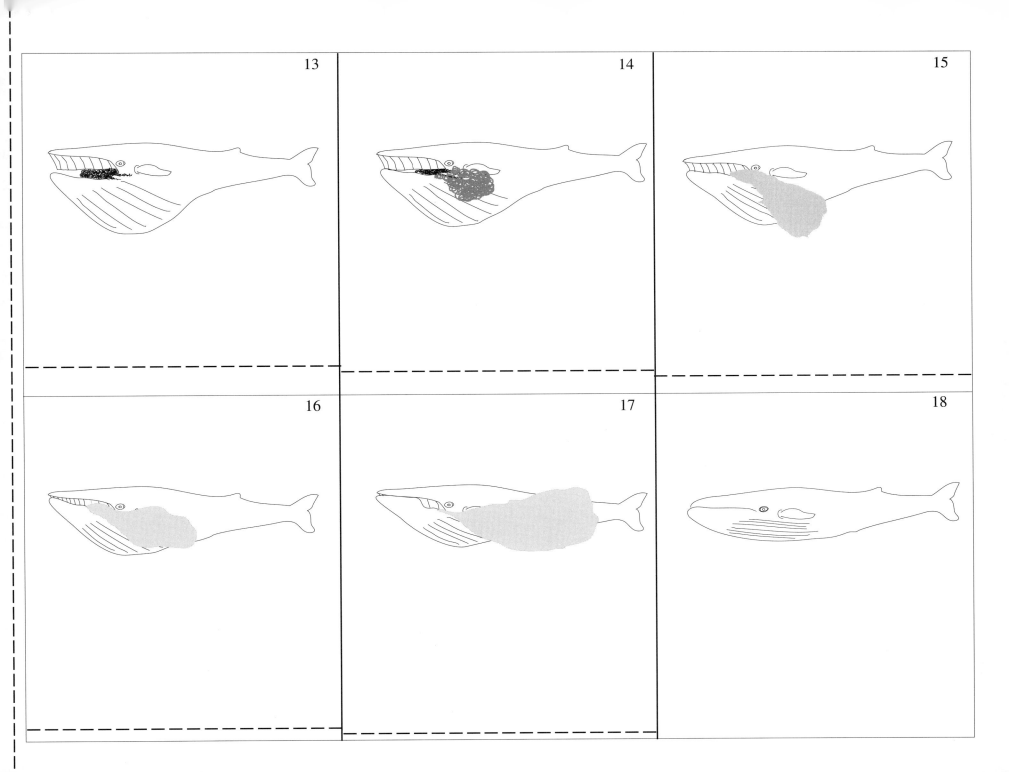

Pick the Predator

So You Want to Be a Whale Biologist

Using the information on feeding strategies of whales (pages 30-31), complete the following activity. The ocean scene on the next two pages has different types of prey, and the cutout page has different types of predators. Choose the predators that would be most likely to feed upon the prey. Cut out the individual predators and paste them by their most likely prey.

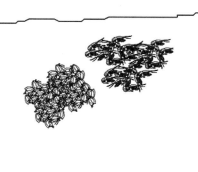

Amphipods

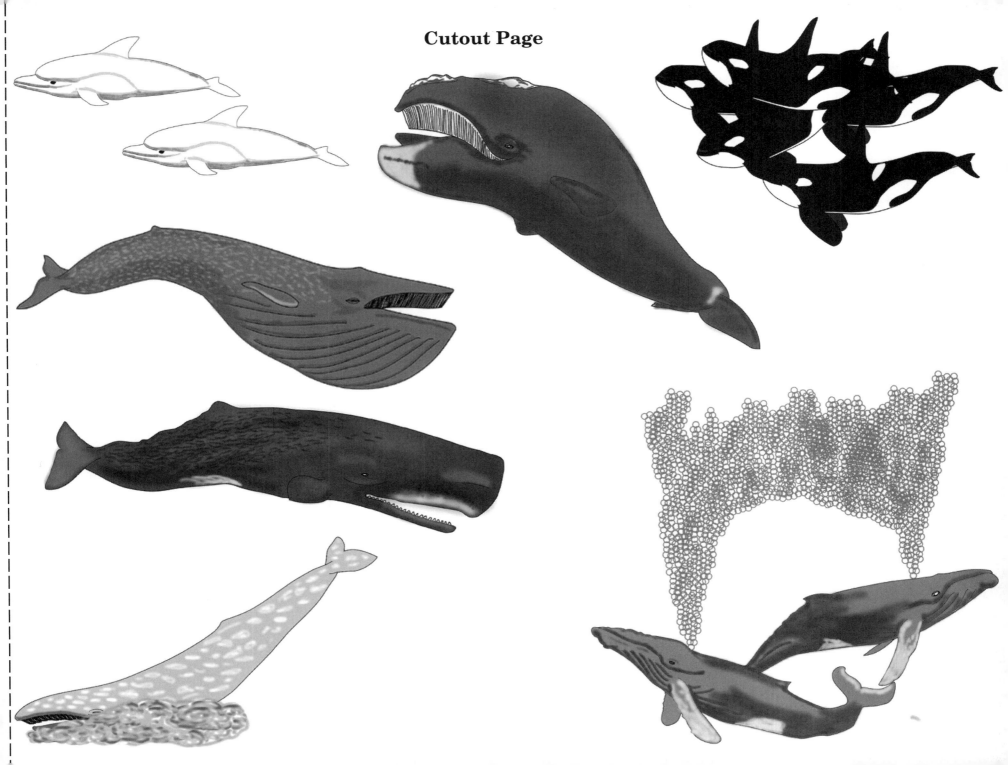

Cutout Page

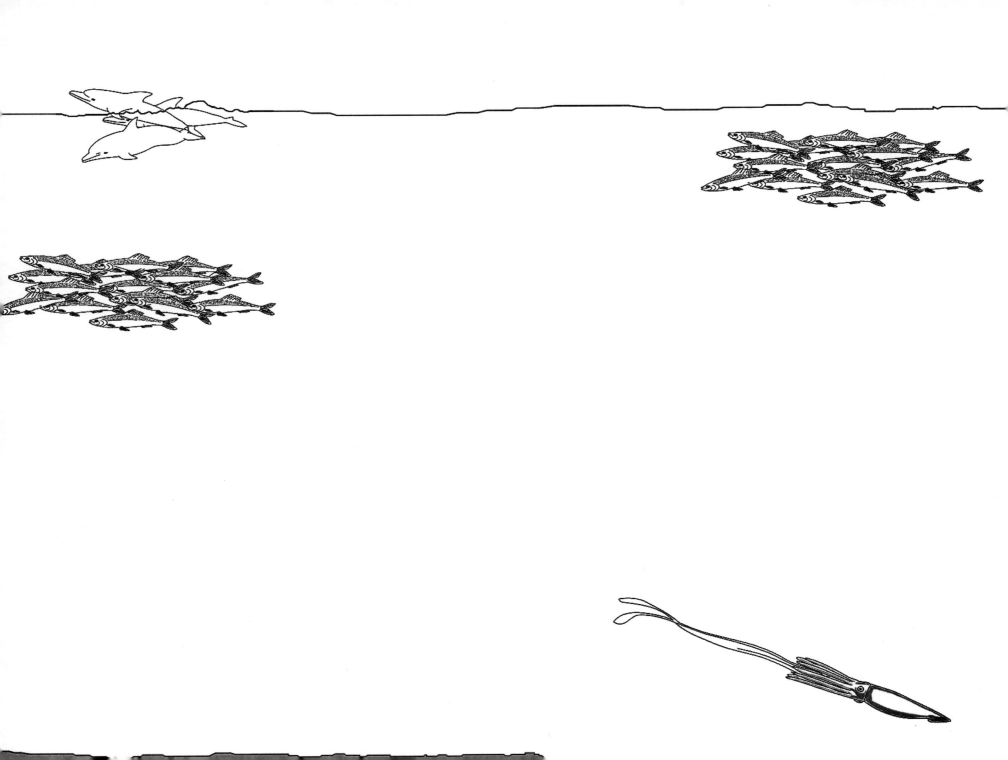

How Whales Breathe

The Old Whale Biologist

The sound of a whale breathing is unforgettable. To me it is as joyous as the sound of a newborn baby's first cry. I'll never forget hearing the whales blow in the thick fog of the Gulf of St. Lawrence River, in Quebec, Canada. At night, I would go to sleep listening to whale blows on the river. The sound reminded me that these creatures were alive just like myself. They had to breathe, too, just like I did (except their breath sounded like a cannon going off or sometimes a lion roaring). It was humbling to think of the power of those creatures compared to myself.

The great blue whale must go through quite a bit of effort just to get a breath of air. It must leave what it is doing at possibly 600-1000 feet underwater and swim to the surface. Its body rolls like a wheel at the surface. The whale positions its blowhole precisely above the water level and expels huge amounts of carbon dioxide, then it brings fresh oxygen into its lungs. All of this happens in the space of several seconds. After several "blows" the whale submerges and goes about its business for 10 or more minutes until it's time to return to the surface again.

I spent a lot of time recording *dives* of whales. The longest dive I ever recorded was on a cold, windy October day in the Gulf of St. Lawrence. We had a trailer set up on a bluff, and when a whale was sighted we tracked that whale wherever it went. It was about 6:15 a.m. and I had the early watch. I was sitting there yawning and wondering why I was up and not in bed sleeping. All of a sudden I realized that there was a whale blowing a long way out in the Gulf (approximately three miles). The whale's blow was angled forward, and it was sitting there at the surface not moving, but just blowing (not typical behavior for a baleen whale). I counted at least 20 blows like this. I knew this was a sperm whale, although I had never seen one. Its appearance matched all the descriptions I had read in whale books. But you must remember, it was 6:15 in the morning (the sun rose at 5:30 a.m.), the window before me was smeared with dead mosquitoes, the seas were

Humpback whale blowhole photo by James Cotton

extremely rough, and this "supposed" sperm whale was a long way offshore.

I started questioning my own judgement. "Am I making all this up? Is there really a sperm whale out there?" Then the whale fluked up (a characteristic of sperm whales) and I let out a scream that would have stampeded a herd of buffalo. As it was, my fellow researchers woke up and came stumbling into the front of the trailer rubbing their eyes.

"What's up?" they asked.

"A sperm whale! I saw a sperm whale!" I said.

I spent the next 40 minutes on the top of a nearby bluff with two grumpy, doubting whale researchers. It was the longest 40 minutes of my life, and I started questioning myself again. My credibility was on the line.

"Maybe I made up this whole affair, and the whale never existed," I thought to myself.

Finally after 40 minutes, the whale surfaced again and all was forgiven.

What We Will Discover

We will discover how a whale actually breathes. We will learn how long different species of whales remain beneath the water. Lastly we will learn how whales are capable of diving to great depths.

How We Will Do This

We will diagram the body parts a whale uses when it breathes. We also will use math to calculate how long different whale species stay beneath the water's surface. Then we will graph the relationship between the length of a particular dive and its specific depth.

Terms for the Whale Biologist

Bends - The *bends* is also known as decompression sickness. At great depths, divers are susceptible to the bends because nitrogen, which is present in the air we breathe, is absorbed into the blood. If a diver swims too quickly to the surface the nitrogen in the blood may form a bubble or embolism that could block the blood flow and possibly cause death.

Blow - The exhalation of a whale is a *blow*. The blow of a blue whale can be as high as 30 feet. It is visible because water (that is trapped at the opening of the blowhole) mixes with the spout of air as it comes out of the blowhole.

Dive - A *dive* is a plunge beneath the surface of the water. When a whale dives, it is beneath the surface for several minutes.

Respiration - *Respiration* is the process of breathing.

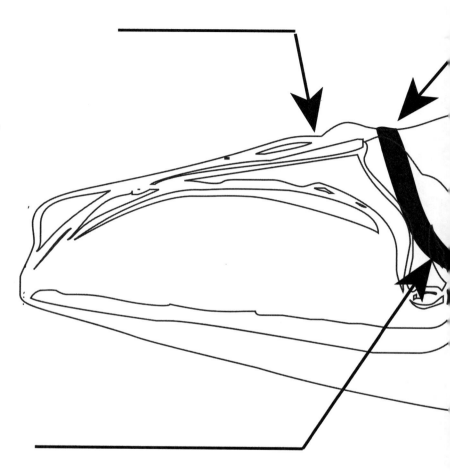

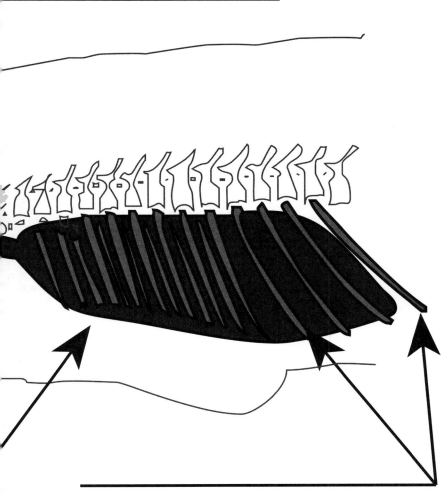

So You Want to be a Whale Biologist

Label the diagram to the left using the following information.

Anatomy of Whale Respiration

Blowhole - The blowhole is the "nose" of the whale and consists of a pair of modified nostrils that open on top of the head. The blowhole opening of a fin whale is approximately the size of an adult fist.

Lungs - Lungs are organs used for breathing. A whale lung will hold approximately 500 gallons of air. Ninety percent of the air in the lungs is exchanged with each breath. The lungs collapse when the whale dives to depths greater than 300 feet, and the air is forced out. Thus no nitrogen absorption takes place during a deep dive and the whale does not risk getting the *bends* when it returns to the surface.

Ribs - The ribs are bones that offer protection for the lungs. The ribs of a whale are much more flexible than those of a land mammal. The flexibility keeps the ribs from breaking when a whale dives into deep water where the pressure is greater.

Splash Guard - The splash guard is the ridge on top of the head in front of the blowhole. As the whale surfaces, water runs around the edge of the splash guard and not into the blowhole.

Trachea - The trachea is the passageway that carries air from the lungs to the nostrils. During a deep dive, the gases from the lungs move into the trachea and are not absorbed into the body. The trachea is 12 inches in diameter.

How Long Does a Whale Dive?

Many articles have been written about length of whale dives. Much of it is inaccurate information. Below is a list of the actual dive lengths of six different whale species. The information was recorded by trained whale observers. In the next activity you will be asked to graph the average dive duration of each of the five types of whales on the graph.

Gray Whale

2 minutes	3 minutes
3 minutes	2 minutes
5 minutes	

Average gray whale dive duration in minutes:_____**3 Minutes**_____

Minke Whale

5 minutes	3 minutes
4 minutes	2 minutes
4 minutes	

Average minke whale dive duration in minutes:_____

Blue Whale

13 minutes	14 minutes
11 minutes	11 minutes
12 minutes	8 minutes
11 minutes	10 minutes
8 minutes	11 minutes

Average blue whale dive duration in minutes:_____

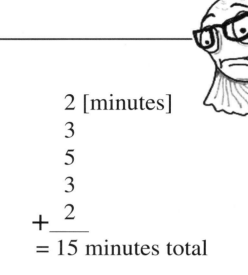

2 [minutes]
3
5
3
+ 2
___
= 15 minutes total

Average = 15 ÷ 5 = 3 minutes

Sperm Whale

The sperm whale is the champion diver. The longest dive observed by a free swimming sperm whale was 93 minutes.

40 minutes	62 minutes
57 minutes	65 minutes
65 minutes	

Average sperm whale dive duration in minutes:_____

Bottlenose Whale

This whale has been known to stay submerged for more than 70 minutes when harpooned.

42 minutes	20 minutes
45 minutes	

Average bottlenose whale dive duration in minutes:_____

Bottlenose Dolphin

The bottlenose dolphin has both coastal and offshore populations. The dives listed below are for dolphins from coastal populations.

4.5 minutes	1.2 minutes
2.5 minutes	3 minutes

Average bottlenose dolphin dive duration in minutes:_____

Typical Depths and Dive Durations of Marine Mammals

Below you will find typical diving patterns of various marine mammals. The dives given are not record depths or record dive lengths for any of the species. The sperm whale is the champion diver of all animals. The deepest recorded dive is up to 7,300 feet. Record the average dive times calculated on pages 48 and 49 for each of the whales and dolphin listed below, and color or shade in the correct depth of the diving mammal. The gray whale is completed as an example.

Species	Depth	Length of Dive	Food
Human	40 ft.	1-2 minutes	pizza
Gray Whale	100-200 ft.	3 minutes	bottom feeder
Blue Whale	300-600 ft.	_____	krill
Bottlenose Whale	1500 ft.	_____	squid
Sperm Whale	3000-5000 ft.	_____	squid
Bottlenose Dolphin	150 ft.	_____	baitfish

Sperm Whale	Bottlenose Whale	Blue Whale	Gray Whale	Bottlenose Dolphin
300 Feet				300 Feet
600 Feet				600 Feet
1000 Feet				1000 Feet

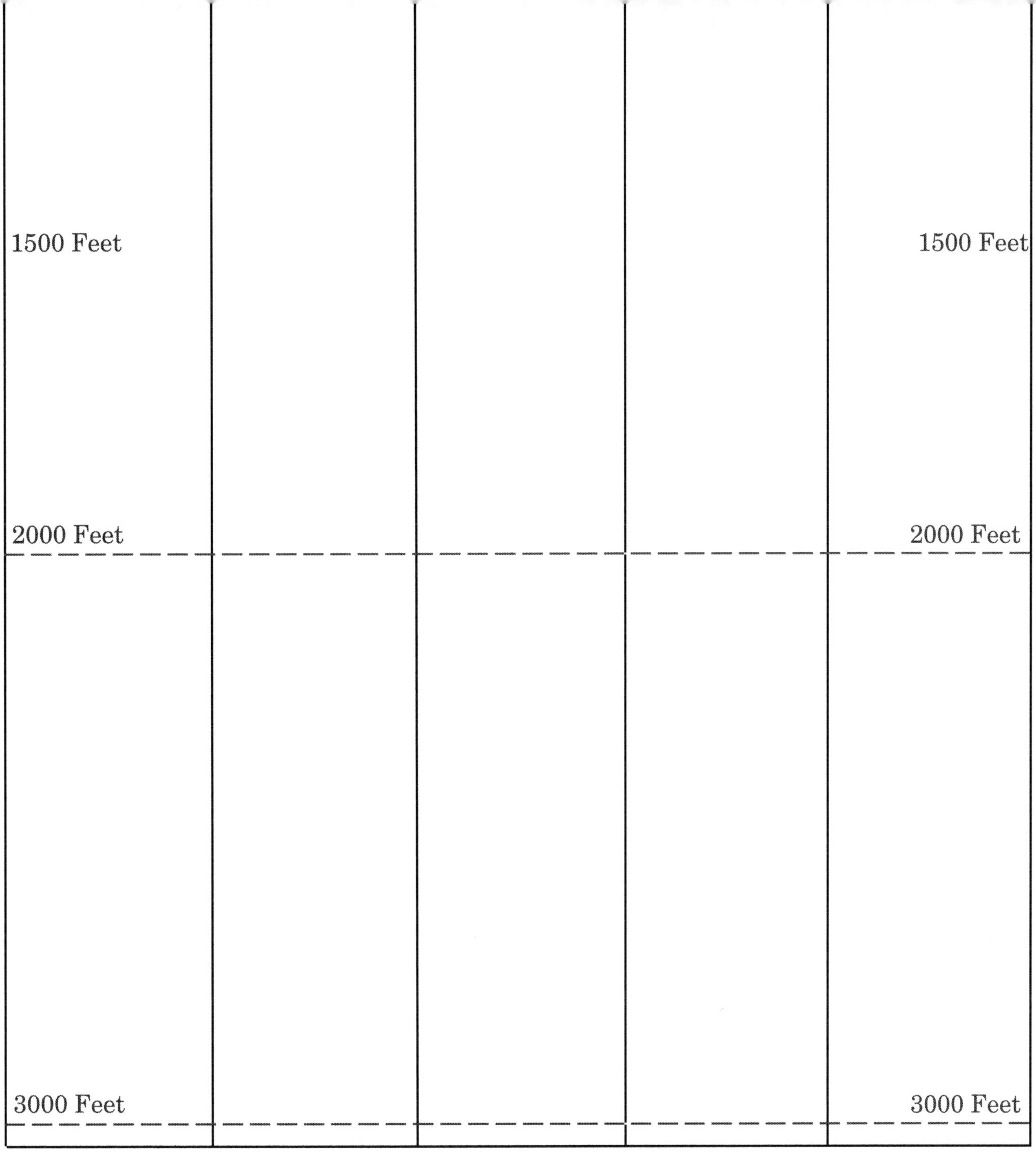

1500 Feet

2000 Feet

3000 Feet

1500 Feet

2000 Feet

3000 Feet

Now, fill in the time each whale spends under water. Shade the portion of each clock to represent the number of minutes each whale dives.

3 Minutes

With thanks to L. Krmpotich, Eden Lake Elementary School, Eden Prairie, Minnesota

Deep & Shallow Divers

Mammals in the oceans have special adaptations for diving. These illustrations compare some aspects of human and whale anatomy and physiology that show how well-adapted whales are to the seas!

In contrast, when whales breathe at the surface, 90% of the available oxygen is exchanged with each breath!

Humans can only dive to about 30 feet and stay for about 1 minute without special breathing equipment.

When humans breathe at the surface, only 15% of the available oxygen is exchanged with each breath.

Heart and Lungs

Small air sacs in the lungs where oxygen is absorbed

Human anatomy provides rigid ribs for protection of the internal organs.

As humans go deep in the water, pressure compresses the bubbles of gas in our bloodstream, allowing more nitrogen to be absorbed into our lungs.

Nitrogen does funny things to the brain. It causes "nitrogen narcosis," which makes a person act like they are drunk. People have done silly and dangerous things while suffering from this.

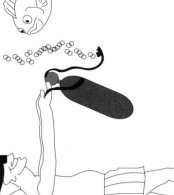

If a diver returns to the surface too quickly, the nitrogen expands because the pressure is less. The bigger bubbles can block blood vessels and cause a very dangerous condition called the *bends*.

N

N

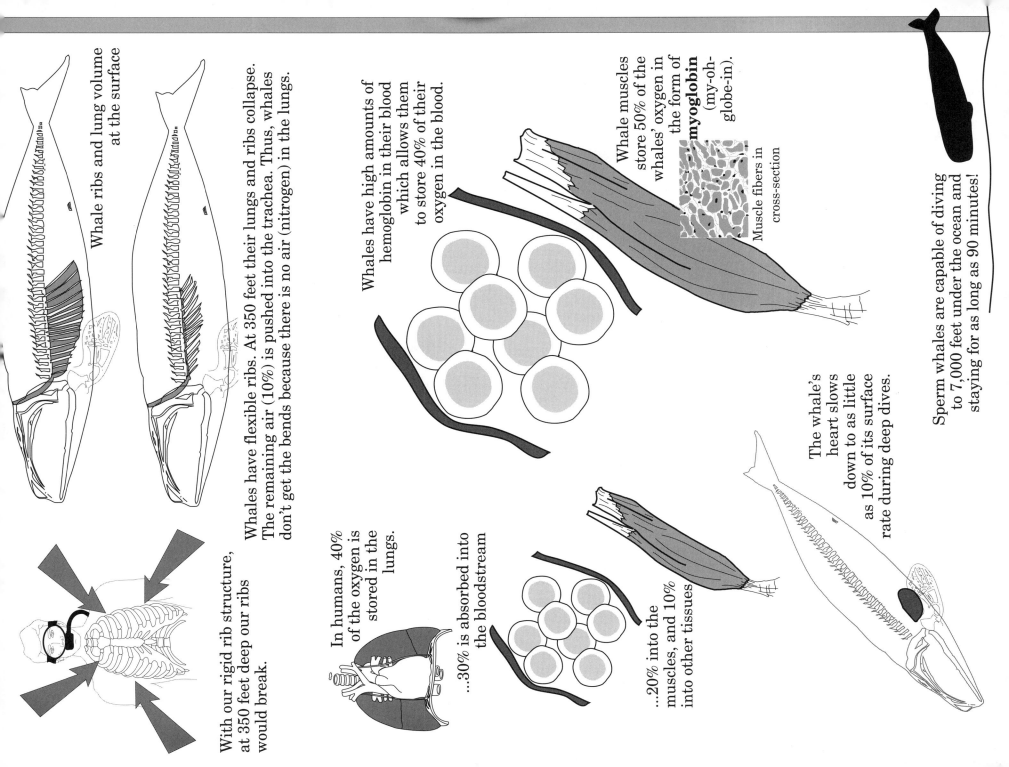

Whale ribs and lung volume at the surface

Whales have flexible ribs. At 350 feet their lungs and ribs collapse. The remaining air (10%) is pushed into the trachea. Thus, whales don't get the bends because there is no air (nitrogen) in the lungs.

With our rigid rib structure, at 350 feet deep our ribs would break.

Whales have high amounts of hemoglobin in their blood which allows them to store 40% of their oxygen in the blood.

Whale muscles store 50% of the whales' oxygen in the form of **myoglobin** (my-oh-globe-in).

Muscle fibers in cross-section

In humans, 40% of the oxygen is stored in the lungs.

...30% is absorbed into the bloodstream

...20% into the muscles, and 10% into other tissues

The whale's heart slows down to as little as 10% of its surface rate during deep dives.

Sperm whales are capable of diving to 7,000 feet under the ocean and staying for as long as 90 minutes!

Up Close and Personal with a Whale Biologist
Moira Brown, University of Guelph, Ontario, Canada

Moira Brown, nearing completion of her Ph.D. at the University of Guelph, has been working on right whale research and right whale conservation issues for eight years, through a nonprofit group called East Coast Ecosystems.

How did you get started studying right whales?
A friend told me about Scott Kraus of the New England Aquarium who was doing a study on right whales in the Bay of Fundy. In 1985 I volunteered as a research assistant for the project and spent the summer in the Bay of Fundy. I haven't stopped going back and that was eight years ago. The right whales in the North Atlantic are the most endangered large whale species in the world. Given the environmental conditions of our oceans and the endangered status of the right whale, I became passionately involved in learning as much as I could about them and working to prevent their extinction.

What skills and personal attributes helped you to be successful?
I was lucky to be born with a good memory, but that is something you can develop along the way. Whale research requires a few life skills, including getting along with other people while living for extended periods in uncomfortable conditions at sea or in remote field stations. The friendships developed in these situations are often very special.

What would you say to a group of young biologists?
Many people believe that scientists—especially biologists—can't make a good living doing research. It turns a lot of people off early on. Don't let that get in your way. You can make a reasonable living as a scientist. You won't become a millionaire, but it is much easier to go to work every day when you are fascinated with what you are doing.

Learn nontraditional skills. Biology majors who can scuba dive are common. Develop skills that make you exceptional, including computer literacy, mechanics, boat handling, and an interest and

Moira Brown using crossbow for biopsy work
photograph courtesy of Margo Pfeiff

knowledge in conservation. Remember, when you study whales you will learn to manage a boat and a research group. You will also be a conservationist and work to protect whales and the marine environment.

What would you tell a young woman interested in being a biologist?
I was out fixing my motorcycle with my niece the other day. She's 13, and she said to me, "This is really strange, two girls working on a motorcycle." I was struck that a 13-year-old in the 1990s would think that was strange, but old traditions die hard and women in science are also still rare. My advice to young women studying science and especially biology is: If someone says, "That's for boys," let it run off your back. If you are interested in any aspect of science and you really want to do it, just go ahead and do it. Keep a good sense of humor about the teasing you may encounter along the way.

Tell us about the proposed right whale conservation plan for Canadian waters.
Since the right whale population is so few in number, we want to provide them with some measure of protection in the areas where they are known to gather as a group. Our research shows that there are two "high use" areas in Canadian waters. These areas are small in size. One area includes parts of the Bay of Fundy (between Maine and Nova Scotia), which is usually occupied by right whale mothers, calves, and some juveniles. The second area is between Browns and Baccaro Banks south of Nova Scotia where many adult right whales are seen in mating groups. More than half of the individually identified right whales can consistently be found in these two areas in the summer and fall. Our biggest concern with right whales is trying to keep them alive. Sixty percent of the population that we have photographically identified has scars from being tangled in fishing gear and another 10% are scarred from collisions with ships.

In these conservation zones, we want to encourage a coexistence between right whales and industry (shipping and fishing). The first priority is to designate the areas where right whales are found. We want these areas labeled on nautical maps, so ships' crews will be on the lookout for right whales. Our hope is that the shipping and fishing industry will be more cautious in the right whale zones.

Whale Research

The Old Whale Biologist

When I first started working with whales, most whale research consisted of carving up dead whales at whaling stations. They were killed and towed to the whaling station where we took measurements and studied their anatomy. In 1972, all that changed when whaling became illegal in the United States. A new breed of researchers sprang up all over the world. These researchers would go anywhere and do anything to study whales in their natural habitat.

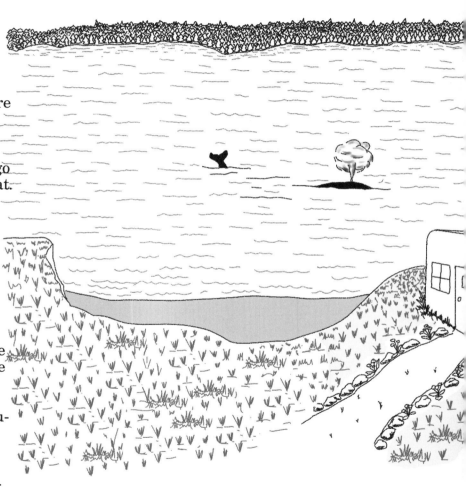

In 1973, I had an opportunity to study blue, fin, and other baleen whales in the Gulf of St. Lawrence, Quebec, Canada. I was young and out to make my mark on the world. There were eight of us living in a small trailer. We lived and breathed whales day and night. It was an exciting time!

Our job was to observe and record the natural *behavior* of whales. Observations of whales are very difficult since they spend 90% of their time beneath the surface of the water. However, it is possible to observe the behavior of a whale at the surface and to draw some conclusions about what it is doing below.

July 16, 1973 is a day that remains embedded in my mind, particularly since it was my birthday. It was on this day in 1973 that we had an opportunity to track a blue whale from 1302 (1:02 p.m.) to 2330 (11:30 p.m.). Just seeing a blue whale will take your breath away because of its size. But knowing that this is the largest creature that has ever lived, and knowing that blues had been hunted to near extinction, made the sighting even more special. We tracked this whale all afternoon and into the evening. It was a window into the private life of a blue whale.

What We Will Discover

In this chapter we will learn more about what a whale does in its daily life by using information gathered by whale researchers. This chapter covers research on migration, estimating speed, and identifying individual whales.

How We Will Do This

We will use actual *data* collected by scientists and develop a *hypothesis* about what a whale was doing or what its speed was when the data were gathered.

Terms for the Whale Biologist

Behavior - *Behavior* is an animal's response to its environment.

Data - *Data* are scientific information collected for the purpose of learning something. In this activity, data were collected to learn more about how fast whales swim.

Dive - A *dive* is a plunge beneath the surface of the water. A long dive by a whale is followed by several short dives in which the whale breathes, is down for 15 seconds, and breathes again. There may be from 5-10 short dives before the whale dives deep for a long period of time. The entire process is called a dive series.

Fluke-up - When a whale *flukes up* it lifts its tail into the air.

Hypothesis - A *hypothesis* is a scientific guess based upon available information.

Migration - *Migration* is the seasonal movement of a species from one area to another.

Radio tag - A device used by scientists to track animals. A transmitter that emits a radio sound wave is fixed to the animal's body. The movements of the animal can be tracked by a researcher with a receiver that picks up the sound from the radio tag.

Information for the Whale Biologist

During the summer months blue whales probably feed day and night, eating frequently because of the abundance of food. There are many things you can infer or assume about what a blue whale is doing beneath the water by observing its surface behavior. A whale is probably **diving into deep water (600-1000 feet)** if it is beneath the surface for a long period of time (12 minutes), if it spouts many times once it comes to the surface, and if it *"flukes up"* (raises its tail) to begin a dive. If a whale is **making a shallow dive** it is more likely to have a short dive duration (one to three minutes), spout one to four times at the surface, and not fluke up.

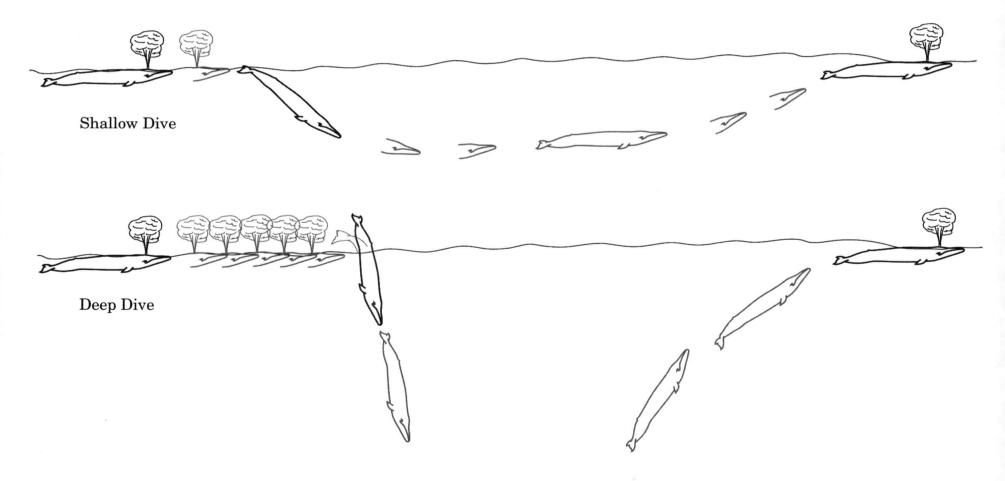

Shallow Dive

Deep Dive

Information for the Whale Biologist

Blue whales feed primarily on krill, an abundant type of zooplankton. Krill can be found in what is known as the Deep Scattering Layer. The Deep Scattering Layer (DSL) is a giant cloud of zooplankton and small fish that can be found at depths of 700-2,000 feet during the daytime. At dusk, the animals of the DSL migrate from the depths to the surface and stay there until dawn, then migrate back to the depths. The darkness probably offers some protection for the animals from their enemies. Many predators of zooplankton, such as herring and squid, migrate to the surface at night to feed.

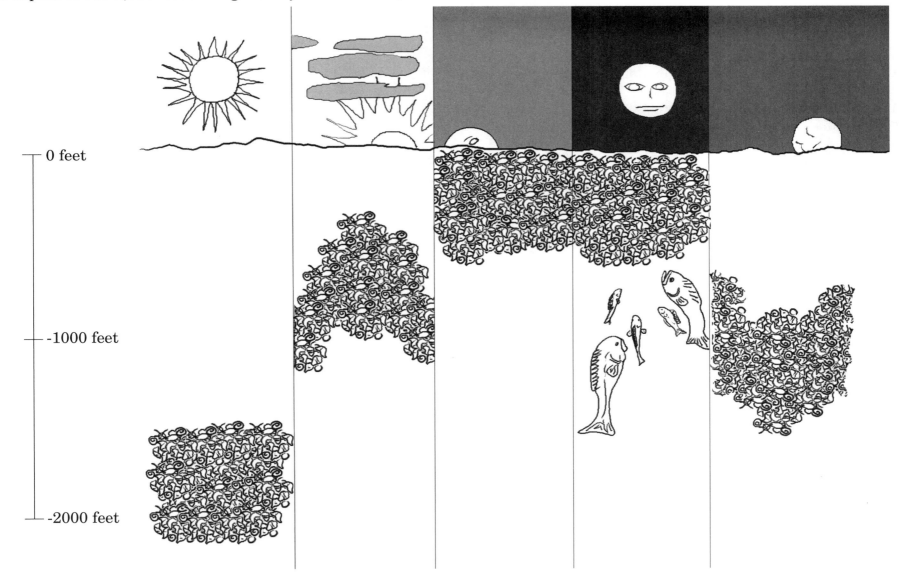

A Day With A Blue Whale

Below are the raw data collected from the blue whale sighting described by the old whale biologist at the beginning of the chapter. This sighting is called **Blue Whale 1302** because it was sighted at 1302 (1:02 p.m.). Your job is to:

1. Analyze the data. You will calculate:
   - The average dive time
   - The average number of spouts
   - The percent of times *fluke-ups* were observed

2. Once you have completed the calculations, determine whether there is some pattern in the *behavior* of blue whale 1302. Then develop a *hypothesis* about what the blue whale was doing during the sighting.

1302-2200 Daytime Observations (1:02-10:00 p.m., afternoon to dusk)
Behavior Observed: The blue whale stayed within a three-square-mile area, but moved around continuously.

Number of spouts	Dive time (minutes)	Observations
10	13	Fluke-up
10	11	Fluke-up
10	12	Fluke-up
10	11	Fluke-up
9	14	Fluke-up
10	11	Fluke-up
8	8	Fluke-up
11	11	Fluke-up
13	10	Fluke-up
10	9	Fluke-up

Average number of spouts:_____

Average dive time:_____

Percent of the time that fluke-ups were observed:_____

2200-2330 Evening Observations (10:00-11:30 p.m., full moon)
Behavior Observed: The whale remained within a half-mile square area and moved continuously.

Number of spouts	Dive time (minutes)	Observations
2	2	No flukes, sinks into water
1	1	No flukes
2	1.5	No flukes
2	1	No flukes
1	1	No flukes
2	1.5	No flukes
1	1.5	No flukes
2	2	No flukes
1	1.5	No flukes

Average number of spouts:_____

Average dive time:_____

Percent of the time that fluke-ups were observed:_____

Create a *hypothesis*

Review the information on the Deep Scattering Layer (page 59) and the surface behavior of whales (page 58). Create a *hypothesis* that explains the radical change in behavior by the blue whale from daytime to evening.

_____

_____

_____

_____

How Fast Does a Blue Whale Travel?

The information for the following sighting was made by the author in 1973. He tracked a blue whale from shore in the Gulf of St. Lawrence, Quebec, Canada. The author moved to different land-observation points (as noted on the map) while the whale was submerged. As a result, a continuous sighting record of the whale's surface activity was made for 2 hours and 20 minutes. At the end of the sighting, the blue whale moved farther offshore, making land observations impossible.

The whale was on the move continually and did not appear to be feeding or stopping.

So You Want to Be a Whale Biologist

1. How to read the map

Look at the map to your right. What do the numbers 0:00, .5, 1.33, and 2.33 mean? These numbers tell you how much time there was between sightings.

The blue whale was first observed from the research camp at 7:17 a.m. (0:00). The whale surfaced for 11 *dive series* during the 2 hour and 20 minute sighting (2.33 hours).

After 30 minutes (.5 hours) it was observed from the Pilot Station (series #4). Series #7 was observed from the Les Escoumin Ferry after 1 hour and 20 minutes (1.33 hours). It was last seen at Au Rocher (series #11).

Use the scale at the bottom of the map to determine the number of miles the whale travelled between the dive series.

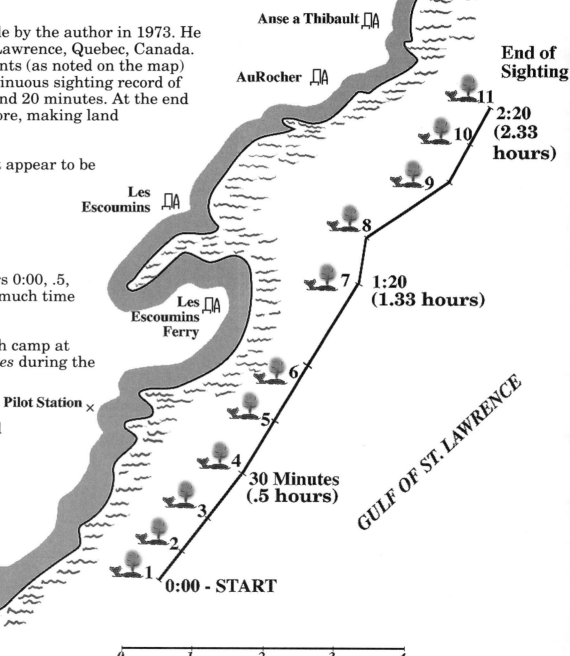

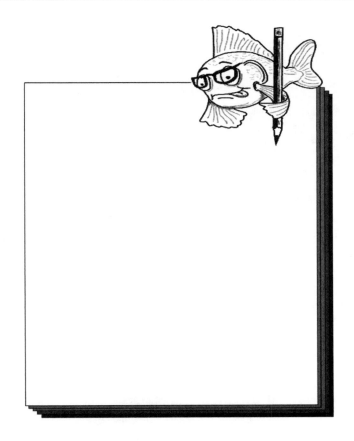

2. How to determine the whale's speed (miles/hour)

a. Use a ruler and the scale on the map to determine the actual distance (in miles) between the start (0:00) and the known time intervals (.5, 1.33, and 2.33). Record your findings on the chart below.

b. The speed is determined by dividing miles by hours. Record the speed on the chart below.

$$\text{Speed} = \frac{\text{Miles}}{\text{Hour}}$$

Location	Dive Series	Time	Distance (miles)	Speed (miles per hour)
Base Camp to Pilot Station	1-4	.5 Hours	_____	_____
Pilot Station to Ferry	4-7	_____	_____	_____
Ferry to Au Rocher	7-11	_____	_____	_____
Totals	1-11	_____	_____	
Average Speed for Entire Sighting				_____

Using Satellites to Study Whales

From an interview with Dr. Bruce Mate, Oregon State University, 1993.

In 1987, the New England Aquarium returned three pilot whales to the ocean after they had been stranded on the beach several months earlier. The aquarium asked Dr. Bruce Mate to put a transmitter on the animals, so that the whales could be tracked when they were returned to the wild.

"Some opportunities are so important that you cannot afford to miss them," said Dr. Mate. He spent several thousand dollars of his own money and took his vacation time to make the project happen. "I place value on research opportunities. It was as important as a house payment or a car payment because I knew that big strides could be made with studying whale migration."

So exactly what did Bruce Mate do? He attached an electronic sensor about the size of a flashlight to the dorsal fin of one of the pilot whales. The sensor recorded the temperature of the water and duration of the whale's dives. The information was stored in a computer chip until the whale surfaced. A transmitter changed the information from the chip into a radio wave and sent it into outer space. In the meantime, a Tiros-N Weather Satellite orbited at an altitude of 500 miles above the Earth. If the satellite was in range when the whale surfaced, it received the information from the transmitter and sent it back to a ground station on Earth. The information, which included the location of the whales, was relayed to Dr. Mate at his research lab several thousand miles away from where the whales were tracked.

What did you learn from this project, Dr. Mate?
"In 95 days, the animals moved 5000 miles. At least two of the whales stayed together and joined up with a pod (*group of whales*) of 100 other pilot whales. We found that pilot whales dive deep during the night to feed on squid. They don't sleep every day. They sleep at sunrise and just before sunset every four to seven days."

In 1990, Bruce Mate attached satellite tags to three endangered right whales. They are the most endangered of all whale species, with fewer than 350 living in the North Atlantic. "The problem for

right whale survival is not whaling," he said, "but whether there is suitable habitat for them. To protect the whales, we are trying to find out what their 'critical habitats' are. These critical habitats may be used for feeding, as nurseries for calves, or as breeding areas, and may be in different geographic locations. The migration routes are important too. We must know where the whales go and what is important to them in these environments.

"We tagged some right whales in the Bay of Fundy, Nova Scotia. Based upon what people had observed in the past, if a sighting was made of an individual right whale and that whale was resighted six weeks later, then it was assumed that the whale had remained in the Bay during that period. Sometimes you don't know what you don't know. Two of the animals we tagged left the Bay of Fundy. One was a female who, with her calf, went all the way to New Jersey. Six weeks later they were within one kilometer of where we had tagged them and had travelled 4,000 kilometers (*2,500 miles*). Therefore, based upon observations like this, we assume that animals may go long distances outside of the Bay of Fundy between sightings. Why would a female with her calf travel such a long distance? We don't know the answer to that yet. But maybe she was showing her calf how and where to find food before they separated.

"An adult male we tagged in the Bay of Fundy made a 3,000 kilometer (*1860 miles*) round trip. But it took an entirely different route to an area 500 kilometers (*350 miles*) offshore, in really deep water (*12,000 feet*). It worked an edge of the Gulf Stream current called a warm core ring that is known to concentrate plankton (*small floating animals eaten by whales*). The male's movement offshore suggests he anticipated good foraging in this area.

"Whales appear to be extremely effective oceanographers. Other whales we've tagged have gone directly into upwelling areas to take advantage of the food productivity there. We have seen them work converging currents and eddies where plankton often concentrate. It's not surprising that whales can find prey in good foraging areas. The question is how do they find these areas: previous experience and memory, random searching, or detecting conditions that attract prey? We are just beginning to see the potential for using satellite-monitored whales to describe their preferred habitats, behaviors, and critical requirements. It remains to be seen, however, whether we will find ways to adequately protect important whale habitats once they are identified."

Up Close and Personal With A Whale Biologist
Dr. Bruce Mate, Oregon State University

Bruce Mate is a professor of Oceanography and Wildlife at Oregon State University. He has conducted research for over 25 years on many types of marine mammals to determine their migration routes, and to study their behavior. His research is innovative and has required a background in engineering as well as biology. His most recent work, tracking of whales using satellites, is an important new research direction for scientists.

Background
I was born and raised in the Midwest. When I was in junior high, I became an amateur radio operator. We had a neighborhood telephone system. In 1958, my friends and I were some of the first amateur radio operators to do a moon bounce. We bounced a signal off the moon so someone could hear it at a different spot on the Earth. Twelve years later, when I got into radio tracking marine mammals I found my background in electronics really helped me.

What skills and personal attributes have helped you to obtain your goals?
I never used to think of myself as a patient person. But for some of my work it has taken me 5 years to have some success. In research I am working for the long term results. I take off chunks of a problem and work on them. I have had to become more organized because of that. Perseverance, organization, and "putting my nose to the grindstone" to get done what needed to be done are attributes that have helped me over the years.

Setting a goal is also really important. There is a line from *Alice in the Looking Glass* where Alice asks the Cheshire cat, "Which way do I go?" The cat says, "Where are you going?" Alice says, "I don't know." And the cat responds, "In that case any path will do."

That is a heavy line. Many of you students feel you are wandering through life. If you know generally where you want to go and you have your antennas up, then you will be sensitive to opportunities

Bruce Mate

that occur in your life and move you toward your goal. In order to change your perspective you have to expose yourself to different people and ideas. It is okay for your goal to change but you need a goal.

On Science and Truths

Most people believe that everything they read in a science book is "the truth." Unfortunately, it is just our perception of the truth at the time the information was written. Scientists don't have all of the answers. But we are continually trying to improve on our descriptions of reality.

One of the most exciting parts of being a scientist is the detective game. Detectives ask a lot of questions and then seek out answers. When I finally get an answer, I may be the first person on Earth to know it. That is a really great feeling! It is like being the first person to climb a mountain. The "answer" may allow me to change my view of reality and make it even closer to what the "truth" is. Truths are hard to come by.

On Luck and Failure

People who look at my success at tracking whales by satellite-monitored radio tags, say, "Wow, that is really neat! Aren't you lucky to have developed this technique?" The Chinese have a saying that *luck is when opportunity and preparedness meet.* You can only get lucky if you are well prepared. An opportunity comes along when you can take advantage of it and that may take years of work. So persistence is important, being there on the edge, and working at it all of the time.

If you were to give a young biologist one piece of advice what would you tell him or her?
If you want to be successful, it will depend upon your doing well in other subjects besides the ones you like. There are some things that you just have to "gut out" (like multiplication tables). If your love is biology then you must be successful in chemistry, math, and physics. Writing is really important. If you can't communicate what you have found out, you are the only one who knows it. It also means that your boss doesn't know it and you won't get a chance to continue what you want to do.

Whale Migration

Information for the Whale Biologist

In this chapter you will be given actual data gathered by whale biologists on the migration of two whales. Your job will be to plot the data on the map provided and to identify specific aspects of each whale's migratory cycle.

Here is an example of how to complete the activity. Below is a chart that shows when California gray whales are seen at specific locations (latitude/long) and notes about what they are doing at that time. Below the chart is a map of the North Pacific. The migration route is already plotted on the map. The following is a guideline for completing the migration routes:

1. Identify the wintering grounds on the map and make a box around the area. Label it "wintering grounds."
2. Identify the spring migration route and use arrows to show the direction of whale movement.
3. Identify the summer feeding grounds on the map and make a box around the area. Label it "summer feeding grounds."
4. Identify the fall migration route and use arrows to show the direction of whale movement.

California Gray Whale

Month	Latitude/Long	Notes
Jan.-Mar.	27°N / 115°W 23°N / 113°W	The wintering grounds of the gray whale (close to land).
April	38°N / 125°W	Spring migration north (close to land) .
April-May	59°N / 140°W	Spring migration (close to land).
May-June	54°N / 163°W	Most of the whales migrate through Unimak Pass.
July-Sept.	72°N / 170°W 67°N / 169°W	Summer feeding grounds.
Oct.-Nov.	54°N / 165°W	Fall migration south through Unimak Pass.
Dec.	38°N / 125°W	Fall migration south along the northern California coast.

So You Want to Be a Whale Biologist

Plot the migrations of the North Atlantic humpback whale and the North Pacific blue whale (pages 70-73) on the maps provided. Using the latitude and longitude given for each whale, identify the wintering area, migration routes, and summer feeding grounds (as shown on pages 68-69 for the gray whale).

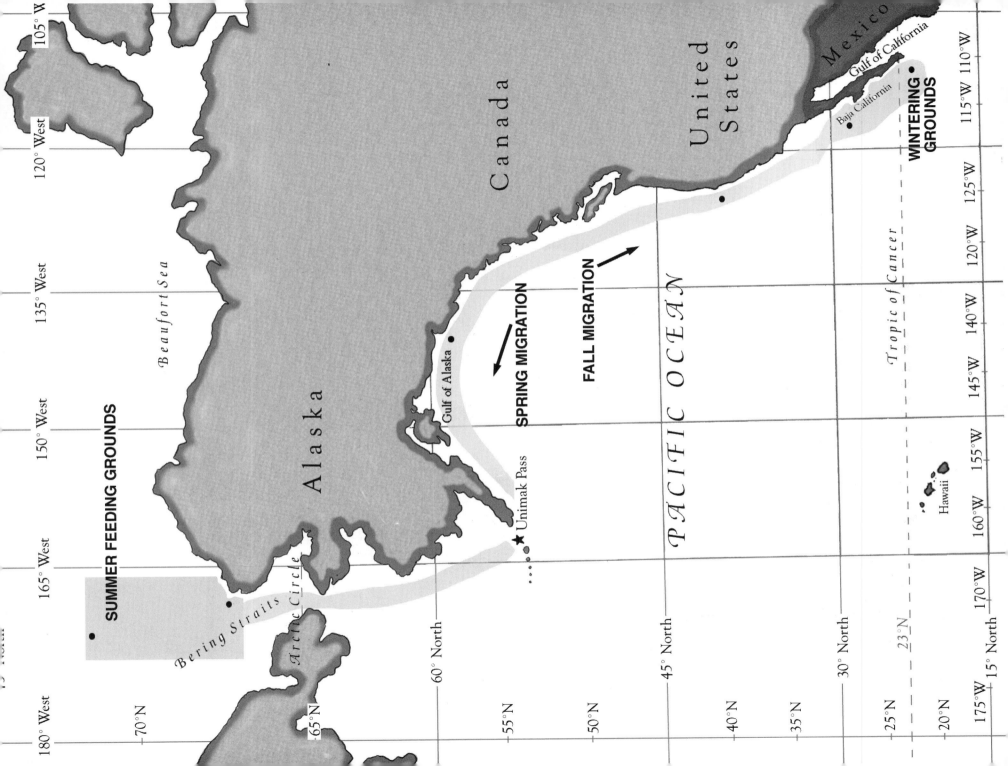

North Atlantic Humpback Whale

The original population size of this species is estimated to have been 10,000 whales and the current one is 5,500 whales. North Atlantic humpbacks are the most studied whales in the world. More than 4,000 individuals have been photographically identified by their tail fluke patterns. The North Atlantic humpback faces many hazards in its summer feeding grounds, including the danger of being hit by ships, being entangled in fishing nets, and water pollution. However, the humpback has been protected from whaling since 1972. Critical areas to humpbacks such as Silver Bank, Dominican Republic (winter breeding area) and Stellwagon Bank (summer feeding area) have been proclaimed *marine sanctuaries* where laws provide yet more protection to humpbacks overall.

There are five summer feeding areas. An individual whale tends to return to the same feeding area each year. However, in the winter, humpbacks will interbreed with whales from other feeding areas.

Month	Location Lat/Long	No. of Whales [Identified by photos]	Notes
Dec.-March	20°N / 71°W	1,305	Wintering grounds
	19°N / 67°W	461	Wintering grounds
	19°N / 64°W	131	Wintering grounds
March-April	33°N / 64°W	115	Spring migration - observed migrating north.
May-Oct.	43°N / 68°W	594	Summer feeding area
	48°N / 63°W	132	Summer feeding area
	60°N / 50°W	155	Summer feeding area
	55°N / 57°W	1,477	Summer feeding area
	65°N / 28°W	20	Summer feeding area
Oct.-Nov.	33°N / 64°W	73	Fall migration south to wintering grounds.

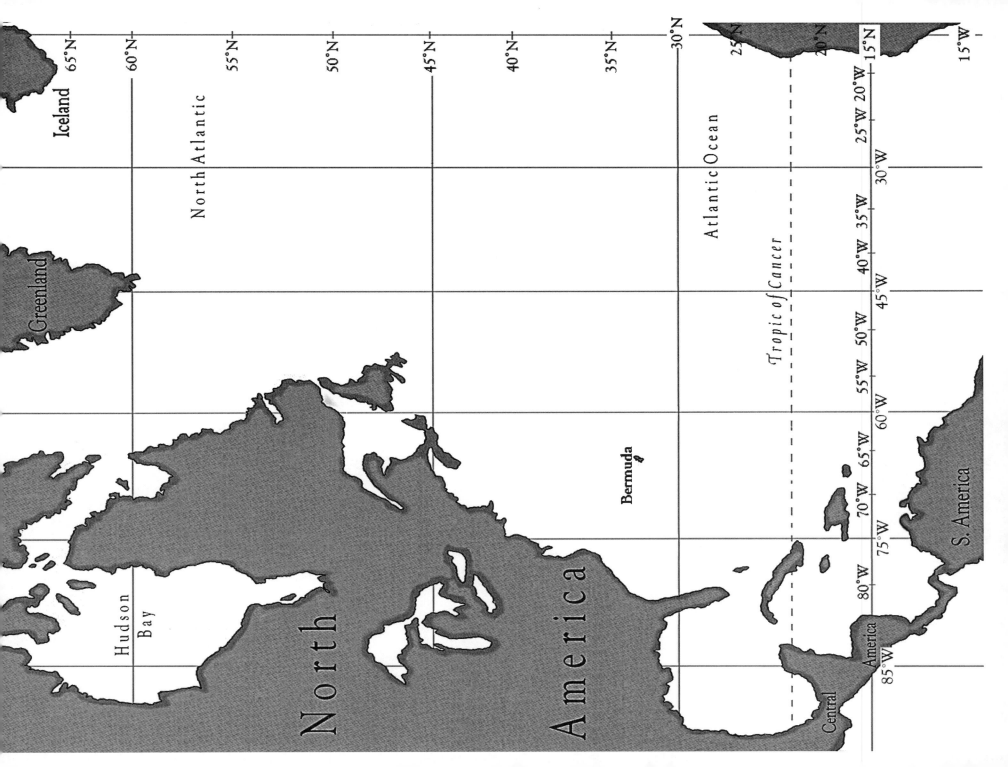

North Pacific Blue Whale

Researchers estimate the blue whale population to be 2,000 whales (1994). Although this is significantly lower than the pre-whaling population (5,000), researchers believe that the number of blue whales is increasing. In 1990, researchers observed 13 calves.

However, since blue whales are usually found far offshore, the impact of pollution, fishing, and shipping has probably been less severe on blue whales than on coastal whales. The blue whale has been protected from whaling since 1965.

The migration of the blue whale is poorly understood because the whale is normally found more than 50 miles offshore. The data given below are from old whaling records and recent sightings of blue whales.

Month	Latitude/Longitude	Notes
Jan.-Feb.*	10°N / 98°W 7°N / 100°W	Possible wintering grounds. Several groups of whales were seen in this area.
March/ April	28°N / 116°W	Spring migration north off the Baja coast. Whales were seen in large numbers.
May	41°N / 130°W	Spring migration. Whales were seen off the continental shelf.
June	50°N / 130°W	Spring migration.
July-August	57°N / 150°W 55°N / 143°W	Summer feeding grounds.
September	50°N / 130°W	Fall migration south.
October	36°N / 128°W	Fall migration south.
November	25°N / 115°W	Fall migration south.

* Sightings made by the author in 1973.

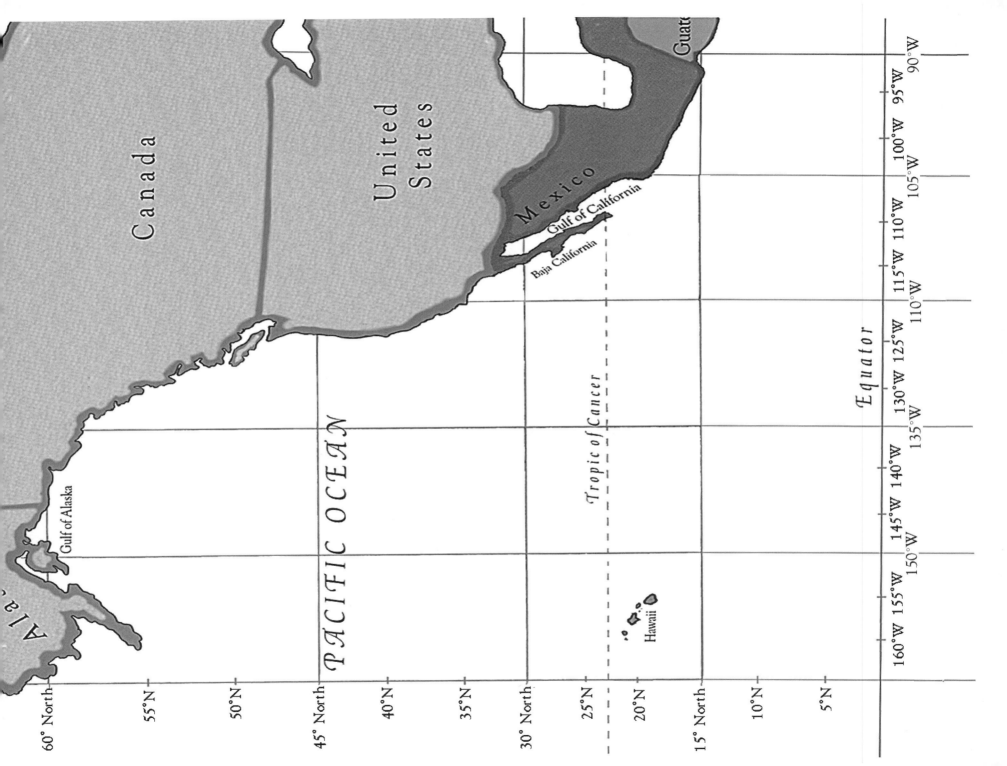

Whale Tails

Information for the Whale Biologist

Before doing this activity, complete the activity that begins on page 70 about the migration of the North Atlantic humpback whale.

The **Fluke Identification Method** that you will use in the following activity was developed by scientists in the 1970s. It was discovered that the underside of each whale's tail flukes has a unique pattern. Using this method, more than 4,000 humpbacks have been individually identified. When a whale is seen it is photographed, and its photograph is "matched" with a photo of an identified whale.

This method has helped scientists answer many things about whales, including:
1. Do whales return to the same area each year?
2. How often do whales have their calves?

Below is a photo of a whale tail fluke. Try to "match" this photo with the photos (Sightings of Unidentified Whales) on page 77. In making a match you will have to compare the pattern of the fluke pictured on this page with the patterns seen on the "Sightings of Unidentified Whales" chart.
Which whale is it?

If you chose whale 6 you were correct.

So You Want to Be a Whale Biologist

Welcome to the whale biologist's lab. The biologist is exhausted from working on her data. See if you can assist her by completing the work!

On the next two pages are posted Sighting Logs of three whales (0054, 0153, and 4040) along with a photograph of each whale's tail fluke patterns.

Also posted on the walls of her lab is a "Sightings of Unidentified Whales" chart. The whales on the chart were photographed at many different locations and need to be identified from their tail fluke patterns.

Each of these known whales (0054, 0153 and 4040) has two additional "matches" on the unidentified sighting chart.

When you do find a match, transfer any of the data (such as the sighting locations and calving information) to the Sighting Log of the matched whale.

Whale Sighting Log

0054

4/76, Bermuda Islands, Migration Route

7/76, Gulf of Maine, Feeding Grounds

6/78, Gulf of Maine

4/79, Dominican Repub., Breeding Grounds

9/81, Gulf of Maine

2/82, Dominican Republic

7/85, Gulf of Maine

Whale Sighting Log

0153-Silver

7/80, Gulf of Maine, with calf

7/83, Gulf of Maine, with calf

7/85, Gulf of Maine, with calf

7/88, Gulf of Maine, with calf

7/89, Gulf of Maine

Whale Sighting Log

4040

8/81, Greenland, Feeding Grounds

Sightings of Unidentified Whales

 **Whale 1**
7/90
Gulf of
Maine
with calf

 **Whale 8**
Scylla?

 **Whale 2**
8/90
with calf

 **Whale 9**
11/86
Gulf of
Maine

 **Whale 3**
3/82
Dominican
Republic
(breeding
grounds)

 **Whale 10**
2/91
with calf

 **Whale 4**
3/91

 **Whale 11**
8/83
Greenland
(feeding
grounds)

 **Whale 5**
9/90

 **Whale 12**
8/86
Gulf of
Maine

 **Whale 6**
11/89

 **Whale 13**
1/91

 **Whale 7**
12/91

 **Whale 14**
6/91
Gulf of
Maine
found
dead

So You Want to Be a Whale Biologist

Now your Whale Sighting Logs are complete. What can you learn about the private lives of whales from your Sighting Logs?

1. What important information can be learned from the sightings of whale 0153 (Silver)?

_____

_____

2. Based on the Sighting Log for 0153, how often do humpbacks have calves?

_____

_____

3. Based on the Sighting Log of 0054, do humpbacks return to the same areas, or do they go to different places each year? (Check the map.)

_____

_____

4. In comparing the Sighting Logs of whales 0054 and 4040, what do these whales share in common? What are some differences between them?

_____

_____

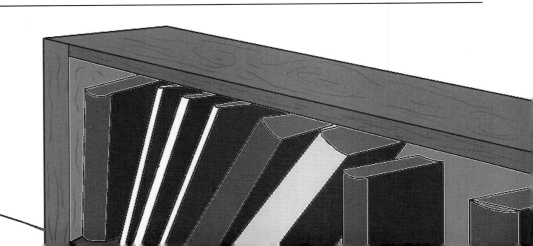

A Year in the Life of a Whale

Information for the Whale Biologist

Read the information below and use the maps to track the migration of the humpback whale. In the activity on page 82 you will be writing your own story titled, "A Year in the Life of a Whale." The following information will be useful in your story.

1. The Breeding Grounds (December to March)

Most of the humpback whales in the North Atlantic come to the breeding grounds off the coast of the Dominican Republic and Puerto Rico. The females are attracted by the deep moaning songs of the male humpbacks.

2. Migration North (March and April)

There are two possible migration routes the whales could take: northwest following the coast to their summer feeding grounds, or directly north through the waters off Bermuda. Whales that follow the coast are subject to more problems from people, since they travel past large cities.

Potential Hazards Facing Whales During Spring Migration

2A. Toxic waste dumps: Waste materials are dumped in the sea because they are too dangerous to be stored on land. Fish and crabs that live around these dump sites have black gills and cancerous growths on their bodies.

2B. Killer whale predation: Killer whales, or orcas, hunt in pods and feed on other whales, including humpbacks. They also eat dolphins, seals, and many types of fish. The killer whale makes echolocation sounds to try and locate food.

2C. Collisions with ships: Many of the whales migrate in shipping lanes. A whale may be sleeping at the surface night or day and not be seen by the crew. Over the years, many whales have been killed by ships in the North Atlantic.

3. Summer Feeding Grounds (May to October)

In the summer feeding grounds the whales feed day and night. During the summer there are great blooms (*population explosions*) of plankton that cause the number of small baitfish to also increase.

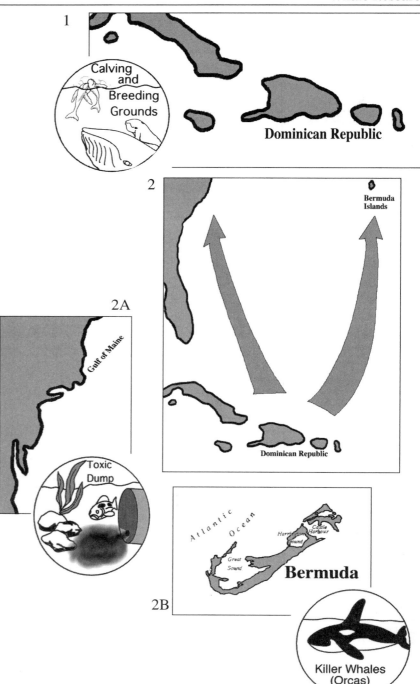

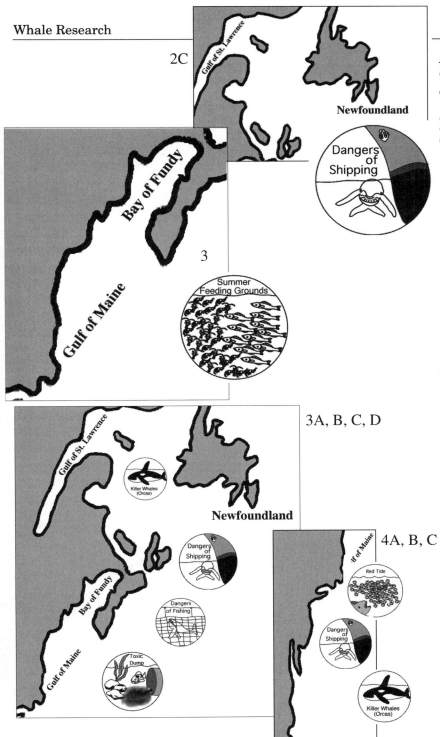

As a result, the whales have plenty to eat! Many whales feed in the Gulf of Maine in the early summer and then move up into the Gulf of St. Lawrence and Newfoundland in the late summer.

Potential Hazards Facing Whales in the Summer Feeding Grounds

3A. Toxic waste dump in the Gulf of Maine

3B. Killer whales in the Gulf of St. Lawrence

3C. Collisions with ships

3D. Entanglement in fishing gear: The summer feeding grounds of whales also support a major fishing industry. Unfortunately, the fishermen use nets that drape deep into the water and whales easily get entangled in them.

Whale watching: Millions of people each summer go on whale-watching cruises in the Gulf of Maine and Bay of Fundy. Boat traffic too close to whales can disrupt feeding or cause injury. Regulations have been created to help protect the whales from whale-watching boats.

4. Fall Migration to the Winter Breeding Grounds (October to November)

The whales follow a migration route south that is essentially a reverse pattern of their spring migration.

Potential Hazards Facing Whales During Fall Migration

4A. Red Tide: A red tide is not a tide at all, but a bloom of plankton that is quite toxic (*harmful to the body*). When fish eat them, they also become toxic. The toxicity builds as it goes up the food chain from plankton to fish and then to whales. A red tide does not occur every year. In 1987, 13 humpbacks were believed to have been killed by mackerel that had high levels of red tide toxins.

4B. Collisions with ships

4C. Killer whales

Now, turn the page and see a map that shows how a whale spends its whole year!

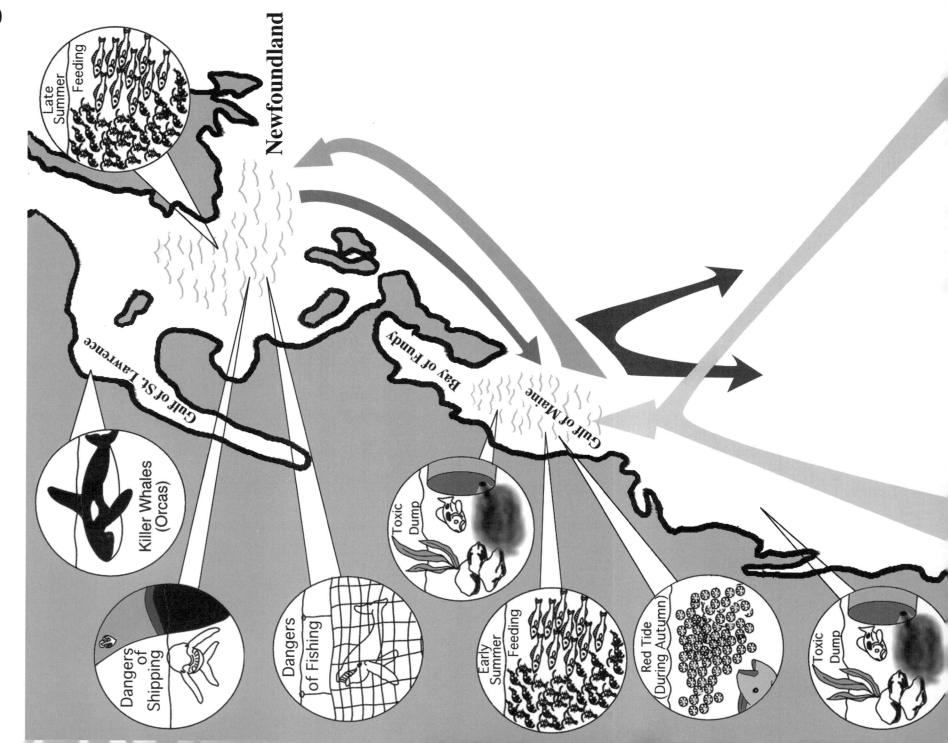

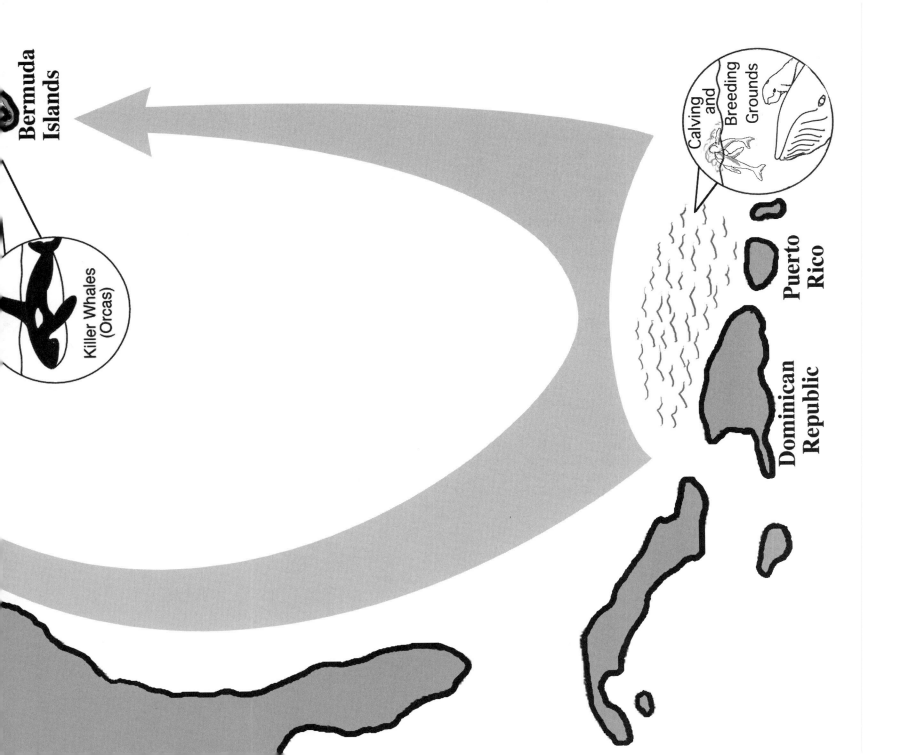

Bermuda Islands

Killer Whales (Orcas)

Calving and Breeding Grounds

Puerto Rico

Dominican Republic

So You Want to Be a Whale Biologist

Using the information and map on the previous pages and this page, you may now write a story about a year in the life of a humpback whale. <u>Choose only the problems that you want to include in your story.</u>

1. Breeding and Calving Grounds (December to March)
Is your whale a male or female? What is its name?

The male humpback sings a deep moaning song beneath the surface to attract females. He will have to fight other males for the opportunity to breed with the female. The male slashes at other males with its tail flukes and uses its head to ram into other competitors.

The female humpback gives birth every two to three years. A cow and calf will stay close together and stay clear of the mating frenzy. The calf nurses frequently to put on plenty of blubber before migrating north.

Start your story with this information, and describe a special adventure of your whale at the breeding grounds.

2. Spring Migration (March and April)
There are **two possible migration routes north** to the feeding grounds. **Choose one of them for your whale.** The map shows some possible problems that the whales may encounter along the way. You may choose ideas from each of the following sections or make up your own:

Orca (killer whale) possibilities
1. Heard in distance but don't get close. *How would your whale react to the sounds and potential danger?*
2. Are within view of the humpbacks, but are feeding on codfish.
3. Attack and injure or kill a in your pod.

Toxic waste dump possibilities
1. Your whale swims through the poisonous waters but doesn't feed because nothing can survive here. *How is it affected? Describe the area in your story.*
2. Your whale feeds and feels sick.

Write Your Story Here...

_____

_____

_____

_____

_____

_____

_____

_____

_____

_____

_____

_____

_____

_____

_____

_____

_____

_____

_____

_____

_____

_____

Oil spill possibilities

Oil spills occur when an oil tanker runs aground in shallow water or rams another ship.
1. Swims through but can't find food.
2. Feeds and gets oil on baleen, clogging it.
3. Ingests large amounts of oil and dies (you or a member of pod).

3. Summer Feeding Grounds (May to October)

Humpbacks often work together to encircle their prey using bubble clouds
(see pages 30-31 for a description).
1. Describe what it must be like to be in an environment with so much food.
2. Describe how your whale feeds on fish and plankton.
3. Describe a bubble cloud feeding experience.

During the summer there are many adventures and dangers that face the whales.

Toxic waste dump in the Gulf of Maine.

Orcas (killer whales) in the Gulf of St. Lawrence during the late summer.

***Whale watching ship*s** in the Gulf of Maine, Bay of Fundy, and off of Newfoundland.
1. Approaches ship, sees faces of people and hears excited screams. *How does it feel?*
2. Followed by noisy vessels, it is difficult to communicate with other whales. *What does this constant drumming of the engines feel like?*

Collisions with ships
1. Sleeping, hears ship, dives just in time. *How does it feel to have a giant ship bearing down on top of it?*
2. One of the whales is hit by ship, injured or killed.

Entanglement with nets
1. Found by fisherman and is freed by a rescue team. *How was it to be trapped in the net and freed?*
2. One of the whales is caught, suffocates, and dies. *Describe how the other whales would feel, watching one of their pod die in the net.*

4. Fall Migration (October to November)

As they travel they can hear the sounds of the humpback whales that are singing in the breeding grounds. The sounds may travel many hundreds of miles through the water. *Describe what it is like to hear whale sounds after a year away from the breeding grounds.*

Red Tide
1. Two whales feeding together, but one is more successful at capturing fish than the other. The one who ate more sickens and dies. *How does the survivor feel?*
2. Many die, but no one knows why. *What should the rest of the whales do?*

You have now been through an entire *migratory cycle* with your whale. This year in the life of the whale included many exciting experiences and dangers.

Up Close and Personal with a Whale Biologist
Steve Katona

Steve Katona is a whale reseacher. He has been a biology professor and is currently the president of College of the Atlantic in Bar Harbor, Maine. The Allied Whale program, which he started, helps scientists collaborate with each other. Participants in the Allied Whale Program have developed a photographic catalog of individual humpback and finback whales in the North Atlantic. The scientific information this group provides is essential for preserving whales for coming generations.

At what age did you first become interested in the ocean? Was there one special event that led to your decision to work as a whale biologist? I think my interest in whales first started when I was 10 years old. I saw a dolphin at Marineland in Florida. Nobody else was near the tank. There was a small football lying on the ground. I threw it into the tank. When the dolphin picked it up in his mouth and threw it back, I was amazed. Only recently have I seen the significance of how that may have influenced me.

If you had a group of young whale biologists in front of you, what piece of advice would you give them?
Spend as much time in the field or in the lab as you can. Develop a strong background in science. You'll need a good working knowledge of zoology, ecology, animal behavior, chemistry, math, physics, and statistics. You'll be able to apply that knowledge to any subject in marine biology. Read a lot, but don't believe everything you see in print. Find out for yourself.

What skill or personal attribute helped you attain your goals?
My ability to work with other people has been important in my career. However, it is also important to take personal responsibility for one's work and to be able to do things independently. Balancing the needs of the individual with broader needs and goals is not always easy, but it is worth doing well.

Realistically, what are your fears for the great oceans of the planet?
Activities such as waste disposal, fishing, shipping, and mineral extraction will never stop. They are essential human activities.

Steven K. Katona

However, they are currently done in such sloppy ways that the oceans (and other habitats) suffer. It is encouraging that so many people are now trying to solve these problems. I believe that committed individuals can make a difference. For instance, almost 2000 harbor porpoises, or four percent of the population, died in gill nets in the Gulf of Maine in 1993. By changing the placement of nets and possibly putting acoustic alarms on them, scientists and fishermen are hoping to decrease the number of harbor porpoises killed.

Pollution is also a tough one. There are hundreds of different types of chemicals that are found in the oceans today. Scientists are getting better at measuring the small amounts of chemicals that are found in the bodies of marine mammals. But it is difficult to tell the effects of harmful chemicals. For instance, harbor porpoises in the Gulf of Maine have high levels of mercury and DDT, but there have not been any die-offs of porpoises. In 1987, when there was a die-off of bottlenose dolphins on the Atlantic coast of the United States, it was not clear whether the dolphins died from natural environmental problems or from the effects of toxic chemicals in the water.

What new projects have you been involved in recently?
I am one of the principal investigators for the YONAH project. YONAH stands for "Years of the North Atlantic Humpback." This was the first ocean-wide whale population study. Thousands of individual whales were identified using photo-identification see (page 68). Project YONAH was a collaborative effort among scientists from England, Norway, Denmark, Canada, Iceland, United States, Puerto Rico, and the Dominican Republic. For two years, the researchers performed field work on whales using the same time periods and sampling techniques. During the summer, whales were studied on the feeding grounds of Norway, Iceland, Greenland, Canada, and the United States. In the win\`er, the whole population was sampled in the Dominican Republic off of Silver Bank and off of Puerto Rico. The beginnings of this enormous project originated in our Allied Whale lab in the 1970s. Our lab is also using photo-identification to document the migrations of whales from feeding grounds in Antarctica to breeding grounds in South America and elsewhere.

Up Close and Personal with a Whale Biologist
Dr. Carole Carlson, Center for Coastal Studies

Early years
My fascination with nature started when I was really young. As a child I always used to look under rocks for creatures and would sometimes fall asleep with leaves in my bed. My mother would say that she never knew what she would find in my room.

What type of research have you been doing?
I have been involved in setting up a filing system for identifying individual humpback whales by using the unique pattern on the underside of each whale's flukes. This method is known as photo-identification because we take photographs of each whale's fluke pattern and catalog it.

At some point we had the whales identified and named, and one of my jobs was to try to match the catalog photos with the photos from that year's field season. In doing so I noticed that the pattern for some whales changed from year to year. I remember going through the catalog and trying to match a photo and looking again and saying, "Wait a minute, this is Talon. Look at that mark. It is dark now." I did a master's thesis on this subject and we learned that the tail pattern in a young whale (up to three years) is not always stable. Although most of the patterns remain the same there is a small percentage that change.

What personal attributes and skills have helped you to attain your goals?
I am a good observer, a watcher. I like to listen. I don't often have preconceived notions or expectations and therefore my perceptions are not easily clouded. I have drive and I am dedicated to the work.

Whale biology has gone through many changes over the years. What new directions has whale biology taken since the ban on whaling?
We have studied live whales benignly (*with as little impact as*

Carole Carlson beside dead humpback whale

possible to the whales) for years but all the time, staying within the conventional framework of science. The new trend is that scientists are realizing that they can make comments about impacts on the environment or about a species and not lose their credibility.

Also, biologists are studying the whales' environment to help them understand more about the animals. Those biologists who are taking an "ecosystem approach" (*studying the whales' environment as well as the whales*) realize that they must be concerned with the conservation of the entire ecosystem (*the interrelationship of animals, plants, and their environment*), and not just the whales alone.

What do you find really exciting about studying whales?
Watching whales grow up and seeing them return with calves. Watching a whale return that we've cut loose from a net. Seeing that whale alive, feeding and healthy. Watching the excitement of the tourists on the whale-watching boats as they head out to sea. The thrill of something so large, yet so graceful. It really does heighten all of your senses.

What could be lovelier than being in an old tall ship and sailing across the breeding grounds of the whales? I remember lying in my bunk and listening to the songs of the whales coming through the wooden hull. I could walk up on deck at any time and hear the whale blows off in the distance. I loved waking up and seeing no land in sight and just whale spouts in every direction.

What advice could you give to young women interested in biology?
Transcend the typical beliefs about scientists. Read books about researchers who are women and have done wonderful work. Pick up Jane Goodall's books or Dian Fossey's books or any of the women who have worked so diligently out in the field. Katy Payne, she is an inspiration with her studies on elephants and whale songs. Their approach to science has not made them less as women. They are not less sensitive...being creative has enhanced their work. There are wonderful women who are doing a lot of field work, directing programs...it is very innovative science.

Break down the scientific barriers and redefine them for yourself. Be proud of the fact that you can be creative and sensitive and have a scientific mind and it can work all at the same time. One aspect does not have to override the other.

Up Close and Personal with a Whale Biologist
Richard Sears

Richard Sears has probably done more research on blue whales than any person in the world. He has had ongoing research projects on blue whales in the Atlantic Ocean since 1979 and in the Pacific Ocean since 1983.

If you were to give a young biologist one piece of advice, what would you tell him or her?
Make yourself as invaluable as possible. Develop your observation skills and talents in electronics, acoustics, mechanics, and driving boats. These are the kinds of things that researchers look for if they are going to hire someone.

In some ways it is bad to be too specialized. If you are a science major, it is a mistake to miss out studying arts, philosophy, and English. Get a good healthy combination of school and field experience. There are a lot of ways of doing that. You can volunteer your time to many kinds of field studies. The bottom line is that you always have to pay your dues. The dues are that you go through college and work for a Ph.D. Or you do research in the "field" and work hard in another way. You have to be very persistent whatever path you choose. That is what I feel inside of me. I remember so many times having been discouraged by an adult because I wasn't doing what he or she had in mind.

The whales give you a lot. I am not talking about data...just being around them. Also, I love to be on the water. I love the sea. I love the changing moods of the sea. (I don't always like being on it when it changes to a bad mood!) There are a lot of really good moments. There is no way that I would trade the last 13 summers for anything else. However, no matter how great a field team is, living and working together day after day at times becomes difficult. But those problems come and go just like anywhere. Often people look at us in wonder and can't believe the perfect life that we lead. We temper their enthusiasm since it is difficult to find much job security in whale research. Somehow the pleasure and the passion that you can get from it compensates for the lack of security. I think one of the difficult things is the lack of security in this work.

Richard Sears photographing a blue whale
Photograph courtesy of Flip Nicklin

Describe your study in detail.
In 1980 we took pictures of the flanks (*sides of the body*) of blue whales and I noticed the spots and mottled pigmentation. We wondered whether the spots would be useful for identifying individual whales. In 1981 we got a confirmation that they would. We had photographs of the same animal from 1980 and the pigmentation pattern was exactly the same. That was when it really clicked.

Over the years we have developed the Blue Whale Identification Catalog. In the catalog are pictures of each individual blue whale sighted by our research team. To date 270 individual whales have been identified from the Gulf of St. Lawrence (NW Atlantic) and approximately 500 individual blue whales have been identified in the NE Pacific.

Do you have any favorite sightings that you can remember over the years?
One day in the Gulf of St. Lawrence, four killer whales came pouring out of the water with a minke whale in their midst. Before our eyes they tore the minke apart, killing it. It took only five minutes for them to kill the minke. They spent about two hours feeding on the carcass, then moved on. That was an amazing peek into a killer whale's life.

In the Sea of Cortez (Baja California), a juvenile Bryde's Whale came over to a blue whale calf, as if it were saying, "You want to race?" The two whale calves took off at full speed. The mother blue whale came barreling out of the water maybe pushing a six-to eight-foot high bow wave while she chased her offspring. We kept up the pace in our boat, probably doing 15-20 knots. That was impressive. She caught up with her calf (who knows what she did to it). A few seconds later they were calmly swimming back to where they had come from.

Since whaling brought the blue whale to near extinction in this century, what are the chances of blue whales surviving the next hundred years or even into the next century?
As far as we know the northeast Pacific is the place where blue whales have the best chance for survival. Two winters ago we saw 13 calves. During our research we have discovered that blue whale females will have a calf every two to four years. One year we observed a female blue with a calf and again (using photo-identification) two years later with a calf. We had another female that had at least two calves in five years. Little by little we are fitting the pieces of the puzzle together.

Whaling and Conservation

The Old Whale Biologist

Years ago, I worked on a tuna boat as a scientific observer, studying dolphins that became entrapped in tuna nets and died. The tuna fishermen on board resented me because I was a "cop" on their ship, "spying" on the fishing operations. The fishermen were concerned about me reporting large numbers of dolphins being killed by their ship. As a result, I felt very alone and was threatened by some of the crew. I decided to work on the project in hopes of solving the dolphins' problems. But after ten days at sea, I was just trying to do my job and not be thrown overboard by an angry tuna fisherman.

One time the net was set on (*placed around*) a large school of dolphins at sunset, killing more than 100 of them. One of my jobs was to dissect the dead dolphins. On this particular night, I worked until 2:00 a.m. with my hands full of blood. Several dissected dolphins contained fetuses (*unborn calves*). I cut the mammary glands of one dead female and the milk squirted me in the face. I thought about the young calf who would probably die because it could not nurse from its mother. I looked at my bloody hands and the dead dolphins surrounding me and felt sick. I was not a scientist, but a butcher, carving up murdered animals. I was a part of the slaughter.

After that "night of death," I resolved to save as many dolphins as I could. I pulled dolphins out of the nets from a speedboat or dove into the nets that were packed with tuna. Many dolphins drown during this part of the operation. So I would climb into the net and pull dolphins out by their long snouts. They were so exhausted and close to death at this point that they willingly let me rescue them. Once, I pulled so many dolphins out of the net that my arms cramped up. I could barely climb out of the net myself and had to leave dying dolphins behind.

I had not done my job as a scientist because the data I collected was not an accurate description of what would have happened on the ship. I had interfered with the operations on the ship by going into the nets. But I had done my job as a *conservationist* because I had done everything I could to help dolphins that were trapped in the nets.

Terms for the Whale Biologist

Break down - A poisonous chemical that doesn't *break down* in the environment will continue to poison animals and plants for generations. If it does break down, it becomes nontoxic and can be used by other living things.

Conservation - *Conservation* is the planned management of a species and/or the environment to prevent destruction or neglect. A conservationist is someone who works to protect the environment.

Endangered Species - An *endangered species* is a species of animal or plant that is on the verge of extinction. Most of the great whales are endangered.

Extinction - *Extinction* means that a species is lost from our planet forever. Most of the extinctions that have occurred on this planet over the last 100 years have been due to the actions of human beings.

Population - A whale *population* is a distinct species of whales that lives in a defined part of the world (e.g. North Atlantic).

What We Will Discover
In this chapter we will track the history of whaling by humans and study the economics of whaling (who made the money). We will learn how whale *populations* are currently doing now that whaling is illegal. We will examine the effects of pollution and fishing on whales, and look at other *conservation* issues facing whales in the next century.

How We Will Do This
We will make a timeline that shows the history of whaling. We will calculate how much money was actually made by whalers. The pre-whaling population size will be compared with the current population size. Finally, we will read a series of informational interviews by whale biologists that discuss various aspects of whale *conservation* and concerns for the future.

So You Want to Be a Whale Biologist

Below you will find the estimated size of whale populations throughout the world. Some of the estimates are very accurate (e.g. humpbacks and right whales since individuals can be identified). But other estimates, like those for the fin and blue whale, are not very accurate since the whales are usually far offshore and are more difficult to find.

Determine the percentage of the whale population that is still alive today. To do this divide the current population by the pre-whaling population.

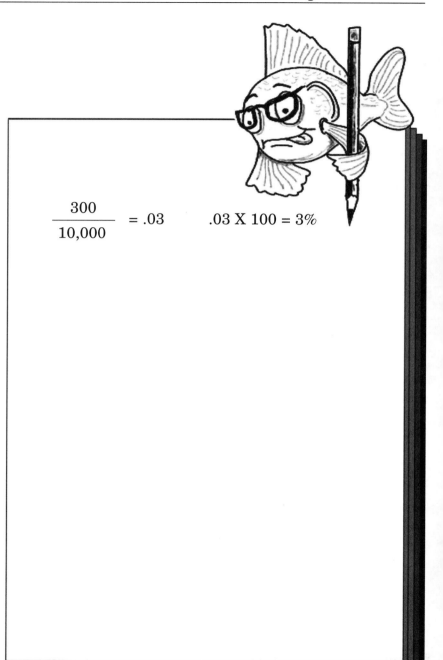

$$\frac{300}{10,000} = .03 \qquad .03 \times 100 = 3\%$$

Worldwide Estimates of Whale Populations

North Atlantic Right Whale
Pre-whaling population estimate: 10,000
1994: 300

% of pre-whaling population ____3%____

North Pacific Gray Whale
Pre-whaling population estimate: 21,000
1870:   4,000
1966: 10,000
1994: 21,000

% of pre-whaling population _____

North Pacific Bowhead
Pre-whaling population estimate: 14,000
1994: 7,500

% of pre-whaling population _____

North Atlantic Humpback
Pre-whaling population estimate: 10,000
1932: 700
1994: 5,500

% of pre-whaling population _____

North Pacific Blue Whale
Pre-whaling population estimate: 4,900
1993: 2,000

% of pre-whaling population _____

North Atlantic Blue Whale
Pre-whaling population size: 1,500
1993: 500

% of pre-whaling population _____

Fin Whale (worldwide)
Pre-whaling population estimate: 470,000
1993:120,000

% of pre-whaling population _____

A Brief History of Whaling

Humans have probably been hunting and killing whales for more than 4,000 years. The earliest records are from 220 b.c. and consist of pictures of successful hunters scratched on stone. Native Americans and Eskimos began hunting whales in canoes with stone harpoons more than 2,000 years ago. These people killed small numbers of whales and used every part of the carcass. The whale was very respected and was the lifeblood of many cultures.

Commercial whaling began in 1000 a.d. with the Basques along the coasts **of France and Spain.** They used primitive rowboats and hand-held harpoons. **They killed slow-moving right whales that were found near shore.** The whalers named them right whales because they were the "right whale to kill." They had the most blubber, did not sink when they were killed, were slow moving, and had extremely long baleen.

Whaling became an important industry because of the demand for whale oil, which was used for lantern fuel before electricity was invented. Only the blubber was stripped off the whale, and boiled down into oil.

Although Columbus was credited with the discovery of the New World, the Basques may have crossed the Atlantic much earlier in search of new whaling grounds. By the 1500s, they and other whalers had killed off most of the right whales on the European coasts and ventured across the Atlantic in search of more prey. The great explorer Jacques Cartier is credited with the discovery, in 1534, of Canada and the St. Lawrence River. However, Cartier recorded meeting a Basque fishing vessel in a Labrador harbor during the voyage and noting that one of the bays in the area was already named Hable de la Baleine (*harbor of the whale*). The peak period of Basque whaling in the New World was 1560-1570. A five-month whaling season produced as much as a half million gallons of whale oil.

The colonists continued whaling during the 1700s. By the 1750s right and bowhead whales were endangered and close to extinction and the gray whale was already extinct on the Atlantic Coast. By 1770, Yankee whalers off Nantucket and New Bedford turned their attention to the sperm whales that were found farther offshore. (Sperm whales are deep divers, often staying submerged for more than an hour.) **The peak time of Yankee whaling was from 1800-1860.** Their ships travelled all over the world in search of sperm whales. During this period, New Bedford, Massachusetts was an important seaport and one of America's wealthiest cities, largely due to whaling profits.

In 1848, the toggle harpoon was developed which allowed the barbed head of the harpoon to pivot as the whale dove, hooking the harpoon more firmly into the flesh. **The development of the bomb lance in 1865** ended the era of the hand-held harpoon. This hand-held gun fired a projectile that exploded in the blubber of the whale eight seconds after being shot. Both of these innovations brought about more efficient killing of whales.

In 1850, whaling on the Pacific Coast increased. The **California gray whale (a coastal species that breeds in shallow water lagoons off the Baja coast)** was the main species hunted. A Captain Scammon discovered the location of the breeding lagoons, and by 1880 this whale was in danger of extinction.

There were three important historical events between 1848 and 1860 that caused the decline of Yankee whaling and may have ultimately saved several species of whales from extinction.
1. The discovery of gold in 1848 lured entire whaling crews from ships that stopped in San Francisco to "strike it rich."
2. **In 1859, the discovery of petroleum and development of kerosene provided a new and less expensive lighting fuel than whale oil.**
3. During the Civil War, the Confederacy sunk more than 86 whaling ships.

In the 1860s the Pacific bowhead whale was hunted by whalers for its long baleen (up to 14 feet). The baleen was split and used for supports in women's dresses and corsets. It is a whale found only in the Arctic. In the Atlantic, near Greenland, the bowhead was hunted to near extinction in the early 1800s. In Alaska, Eskimos had been hunting it for more than a thousand years but had made little impact on its population size. With the arrival of American whalers in 1848, more than 15,000 bowheads were killed in just 20 years. Alaska was a very dangerous whaling ground. More than 150 whale ships were trapped and crushed by ice. By 1900 the Alaskan bowhead was close to extinction. When a substitute for baleen was invented (spring steel), the price of baleen for women's corsets and dresses dropped from five dollars a pound to fifty cents a pound. When the price for baleen dropped, the whalers stopped coming to hunt in Alaska and the few remaining bowheads were saved from extinction.

Up until 1880 there was one family of whales that was virtually unharmed by this onslaught of death, the *Balaenopteridae*, which includes the **blue and fin whales.** They were too large, too fast, and they sank when killed. In 1890 a Norwegian whaler named Sven Foyn changed their fate. **He used a faster steam-driven vessel that had a cannon-like harpoon gun mounted on the bow.** When a whale was killed, a long tube was pushed into the body cavity of the animal, and compressed air was pumped into it to keep it afloat. With this invention the blue and fin whales became part of the slaughter.

In 1900, **Antarctica was discovered to be the greatest whaling grounds in the world.** It had thousands of blue, fin, and humpback whales that had never been hunted. The main whaling base was set up on South Georgia Island south of Argentina.

The year 1925 saw the development of the factory ship. Whalers modified the stern (*rear of a ship*) with a ramp, so a whale could be dragged onto the deck with a winch and flensed (*cut up in pieces*). Catcher boats with cannon harpoons were mounted on the bow (*front of the ship*) and were used to kill the whales. The dead whales were towed by the catcher boats back to the factory ship to be processed. With the development of the factory ship, whalers could go anywhere in the open sea to hunt whales.

In the Antarctic, from 1925 to 1935, there was the greatest slaughter of whales that had ever occurred. Some 40,000 were killed in 1931 alone, 29,000 of which were blue whales.

In 1929, the first whale protection law was passed. It prohibited all hunting of right whales. In 1936, a similar law protected the grays. This was passed just in time since the Pacific gray whale population had declined to a dangerous low of only 4,000.

Whalers from all over the world realized that their industry was in danger of collapsing. In an effort to regulate the number of whales killed, they **established the International Whaling Commission in 1946.** It took more than ten years for the International Whaling Commission to pass a resolution protecting the blue whale. This finally happened in 1965, when the blue whale numbers were so low that the whalers could no longer find any to kill.

In 1970, people started thinking differently about whales. Roger Payne recorded *Songs of the Humpback Whale.* Millions of his recordings were sold. Greenpeace, a conservation organization, began following whalers on the open seas and disturbed their whaling operations. **The Save the Whales Campaign developed.** Millions of adults and schoolchildren wrote letters to Congress urging them to protect whales and ban all whale hunting in the United States. **In 1972, the United States became the first country in the world to protect all whales, dolphins, and seals**. However, whales were dying in other parts of the world. Over the next ten years many other countries passed similar laws. **In 1986, a worldwide ban on whaling was passed by the International Whaling Commission**. As of 1995, three countries, **Japan, Iceland, and Norway,** have not agreed to the ban on whaling. They continue what they call **"scientific whaling" on the smallest of baleen whales, the minke.** Minkes had never been hunted previously since they are so small. The highly suspect "scientific whaling" apparently involves making a few measurements before the whales are processed for human consumption.

So You Want to Be a Whale Conservationist

Fill in the missing information on the whaling timeline on the next two pages. Refer back to the text when necessary.

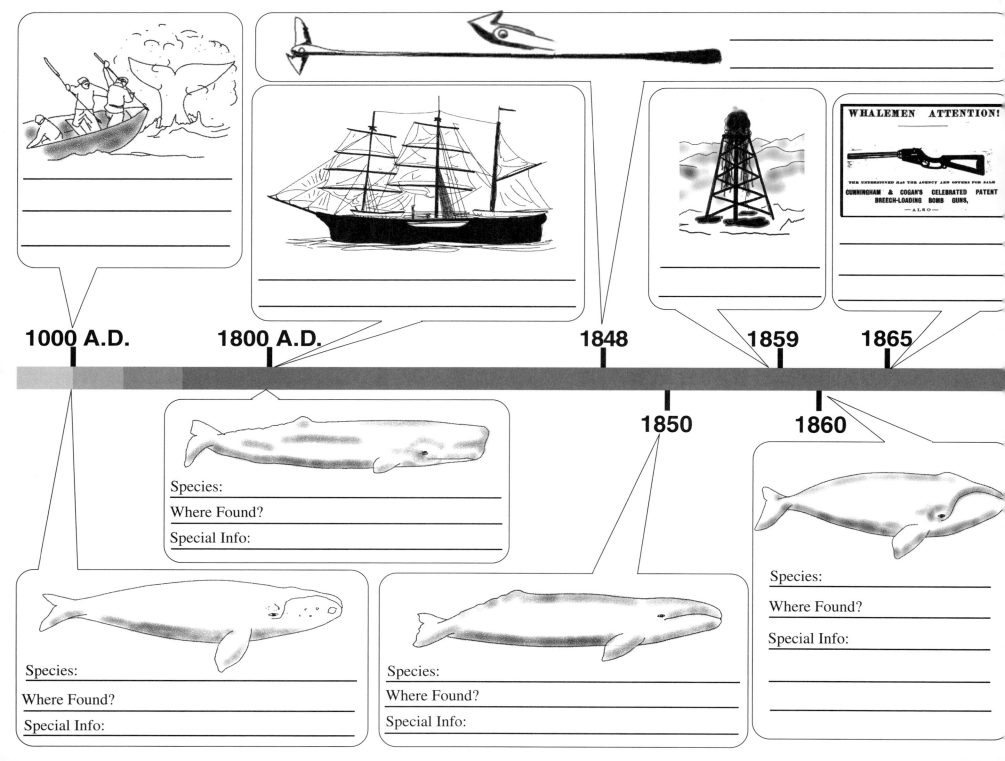

WHALEMEN ATTENTION!

THE UNDERSIGNED HAS THE AGENCY AND OFFERS FOR SALE
CUNNINGHAM & COGAN'S CELEBRATED PATENT
BREECH-LOADING BOMB GUNS,
—ALSO—

1000 A.D.

1800 A.D.

1848

1859

1865

1850

1860

Species: _____
Where Found? _____
Special Info: _____

Species: _____
Where Found? _____
Special Info: _____

Species: _____
Where Found? _____
Special Info: _____

Species: _____
Where Found? _____
Special Info: _____

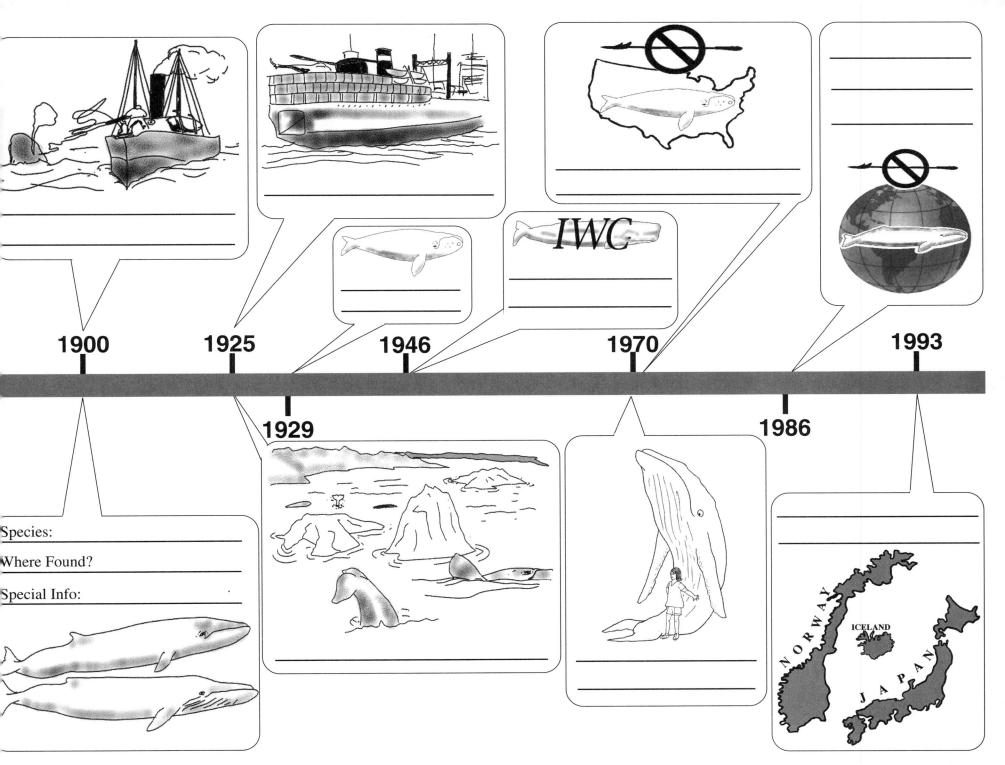

1900

1925

1929

Species: _____

Where Found? _____

Special Info: _____

1946

IWC

1970

1986

1993

NORWAY

ICELAND

JAPAN

Why Were Whales Hunted?

The heyday of American or Yankee whaling was from 1800-1860. The whaling fleet sprung from two New England ports: New Bedford and Nantucket, Massachusetts. In 1848 these were two of the wealthiest cities in the United States. The Yankee whaling fleet had as many as 735 ships and employed as many as 20,000 men. A voyage often took two years and visited such far-off places as Hawaii, Africa, and Australia. The whalers hunted primarily sperm whale for the oil found in its head. The oil was used for smokeless candles (the primary source of lighting during this period) and lubrication of machinery. They also hunted the now-rare right whale for its oil and baleen (*whalebone*). The baleen was used by the women's garment industry.

It is important to know that the price of whale products changed from year to year. If the amount of oil or whalebone on the market exceeded the demand by consumers, then the price decreased.

So You Want to Be a Whale Biologist

In order to understand why whaling was such an important industry, you will calculate how much money was actually made by the *Lagoda*, a Yankee whale ship in 1843. Also, you will calculate who benefited most from this industry.

The *Lagoda* sailed into New Bedford loaded with the following materials:

600 barrels of sperm whale oil
2,700 barrels of whale oil (rendered from blubber)
17,000 pounds of baleen (whalebone)

There were 32 gallons in each barrel.
The price for whale products was up in 1843. Following are the prices that were actually paid:

$ 1.25 per gallon for sperm whale oil
$ .43 per gallon for whale oil
$ .31 cents per pound for whalebone

600 barrels of sperm whale oil

X 32 gallons per barrel

= 19,200 gallons

19,200 gallons of sperm whale oil

X $1.25 per gallon

= $24,000 for the trip in sperm whale oil alone!

1.What was the total value of whale products on the ship in 1843?

Sperm Whale Oil_____**$24,000** (see example to the left)_____

Whale Oil_____

Baleen (Whalebone)_____

Total value_____

2. The value of the dollar in 1995 is much less than it was in 1843. How much would the ship's cargo be worth using a 1995 dollar? (Twenty dollars in 1995 is equivalent to one dollar in 1843.)

_____

Now calculate the individual shares of the crew aboard the ship.

3. The owner got 2/3 of what was brought in:

His share in 1843_____

The value of his share in 1995_____

4. The captain got 1/8 of what was brought in:

His share in 1843_____

The value of his share in 1995 _____

5. A seaman got 1/150 of what was brought in:

His share in 1843_____

The value of his share in 1995_____

Whale Baleen and Women's Corsets

The bowhead whale is an Arctic whale that has extremely long baleen (up to 14 feet). It was hunted to near extinction in Greenland to supply the women's garment industry with baleen. The baleen was flexible and was used in making women's dresses and corsets. In 1848, a new bowhead whaling ground was discovered in the Arctic Pacific off the coast of Alaska. Word spread like wildfire. Just as a gold strike attracts prospectors, whaling ships flocked into the area to hunt bowheads. For 20 years the bowheads were savagely hunted until they were almost eliminated. Hunting whales in the Arctic was an extremely dangerous and costly venture. In September 1871, 39 whaling ships were trapped by ice and had to be abandoned. All of the crew escaped, but the oil and whalebone (valued at $1.5 million in 1871) were lost. **In 1850, when the whales were bountiful, the price of whalebone was 31 cents a pound, and 3,654,000 pounds of whalebone were harvested.**

As the whales became more and more rare the price was driven up by the demand from the women's garment industry. **In 1900, the price of baleen got as high as five dollars a pound as an incentive to keep whalers hunting the bowheads.**

In 1909 spring steel was invented. It was cheaper and more accessible than baleen. Spring steel replaced baleen in the manufacture of women's corsets. **As a result the price of baleen dropped to 50 cents a pound.** The bowhead whale was saved from extinction. No Yankee whalers returned to the Arctic after 1909.

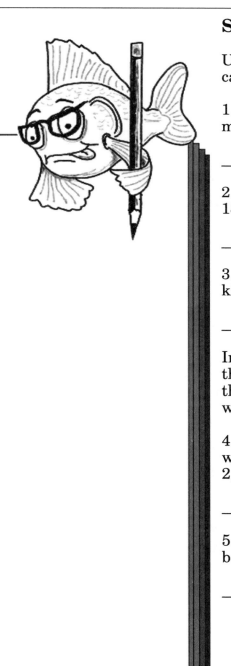

So You Want to Be a Whale Biologist

Use the information from "Whale Baleen and Women's Corsets" to calculate the following information:

1. The baleen of one bowhead whale weighed 2,200 pounds. How many bowhead whales were killed in 1850?

_____

2. How much was the baleen from one bowhead whale worth in 1850?

_____

3. How much money was made from the baleen of all the bowheads killed in 1850?

_____

In 1900, the price of baleen skyrocketed because the demand from the garment industry was high while bowhead whales were rare. At this time, the whales were being killed only for their baleen. The oil was not even used by the whalers.

4. Calculate how much the baleen was worth from one bowhead whale in 1900. (Remember: the baleen from one bowhead weighed 2,200 pounds.)

_____

5. Then in 1909 the price of baleen dropped. How much was the baleen worth from one bowhead whale in 1909?

_____

Can the North Atlantic Right Whale Survive the Next 50 Years?

The North Atlantic right whale has been hunted for hundreds of years by whalers. Its population size has been conservatively estimated at 10,000 before whaling began and as low as 50 animals in the early 1900s. Since 1935 very few right whales have been hunted, yet the population today is no higher than 350 animals. New dangers threaten the survival of the North Atlantic right whale. Eleven percent of the identified individuals in the population have scars from being struck by ships, while 58% of the whales have scars from entanglement with ropes and nets of fishing gear. Marine pollution is another danger which could cause the right whales to become extinct.

So You Want to Be a Whale Biologist

The following activity was developed to show how difficult it will be for right whales to recover from the damage of whaling. The events given for this activity have not actually happened. But the data presented are similar to what researchers have found about right whales.

In this study you will track the growth of the right whale population over four years. Year 1 has been completed as an example. The population size at the beginning of Year 1 is 300 whales. Five percent of the population gives birth, increasing the population by 15. Throughout the year 1.5% of the animals die of old age or by killer whale attacks (decreasing the population by four). Another 1.5% die in net entanglements or are struck by ships (decreasing the population by four). At the end of the year the population has only increased by seven whales. Calculate the growth (or decrease) over the next three years.

Year 1

Population size:	**300 whales**
5% have calves (300 x .05 = 15)	**+** 15
1.5% die from natural causes (300 x .015 = ~4)	**-** 4
1.5% die from entanglement in nets or are struck by ships (300 x .015 = ~4)	**-** 4
Number of whales at the end of year:	**307**

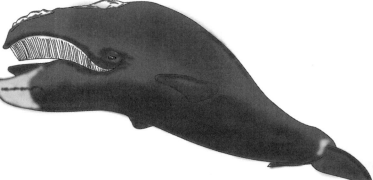

Year 2 Population Size: 307 **Whales**

4% have calves   (307 x .04 = _____)   **+** _____
1% die from natural causes   (307 x _____ = _____)   **-** _____
2% die from entanglements and ships   (_____ x .02 = _____)   **-** _____

Population at the end of year: _____ **Whales**

Year 3 Population Size: _____ **Whales**

The National Fisheries Service passes several laws to protect right whales from being struck by ships and entangled in fishing nets.
6% have calves   (_____ x _____ =)   **+** _____
1% die from natural causes   (_____ x _____ =)   **-** _____
0 die from entanglements and ships   **-**   0

Population at the end of year: _____ **Whales**

Year 4 Population Size: _____ **Whales**

5% have calves   (_____ x _____ =)   **+** _____
1% die from natural causes   (_____ x _____ =)   **-** _____
0 die from entanglements or ships   **-**   0
10% die from a major oil spill in the right whale feeding grounds   (_____ x _____ =)   **-** _____

Population at the end of year: _____ **Whales**

Analysis:

1. After years 1 and 2, how would you describe the population growth?

_____

2. In year 3, how did the conservation measures affect population growth?

_____

3. What effect would a major environmental disaster (oil spill, marine pollution) have on the right whale population?

_____

Up Close and Personal with a Whale Researcher
Amy Knowlton, New England Aquarium Right Whale Researcher

What do you find exciting about your career?
I like being on the forefront of knowledge gathered about right whales.
Every little piece of information we learn about right whales helps us
identify factors limiting their recovery and enables us to recommend
sensible protection measures for this species.

Being at sea is a fascinating part of the job for me. The sea is one of the
few places that I can get away from all the distractions of daily life and
really focus on the research.

What is the most exciting observation you have witnessed at sea?
Mating right whales! Based on our underwater recordings, we believe
the female is in control of the mating situation. The female appears to be
the only one vocalizing (in effect calling the males in). The males must
compete with each other to mate with her. So ideally she will mate with
the male that is most fit (*strongest*).

One of the most interesting events I witnessed was a large mating group
of about 30 right whales. It was very active with water churning and 40-
ton whales rolling this way and that. Twenty-nine males all trying to
mate with one female! We were listening to her underwater vocalizations on the hydrophone (*an instrument for listening to underwater
sounds*) and all of a sudden the sounds stopped. At that instant all of the
whales were under the surface of the water, not visible to us. After a
minute or two, all the males started coming to the surface and milling
about. The action had stopped. It became clear to us that the female had
stopped vocalizing and had taken off, leaving the males to wonder where
she had gone!

What skills and personal attributes have helped you to attain your goals?
Right whales are not predictable, therefore the job is not predictable.
Flexibility is very important as well as having a good sense of humor if
things are not going the way they were planned. These are two important attributes for field research.

Two skills that initially helped me obtain this job (which started as a

Amy Knowlton

volunteer position) were boat handling and cartography (*map making*).

Is there any part of your work that you don't like, but still must do?
It is essential that a scientist pay attention to details in order to obtain reliable data. There is no denying that the work gets tiresome. The process of analyzing our right whale data is often monotonous: inputting data into the computer, "matching" the slides (*identifying individual whales from markings seen on slides*), and doing the paperwork. However, it is the most important part of our research. It is during the analysis that we make most of our discoveries about these whales.

There is an element of danger in doing any field research. I have had several close calls including a plane crash at sea, a shipwreck, and being nearly run down by a freighter. However, I do not believe in letting fears about potential danger interfere with what I love doing most (which is being at sea). It is wise to be cautious and safety conscious, but not paranoid!

Perhaps the hardest part of this work occurs when a right whale dies. I feel a deep sense of loss when I witness a dead right whale, especially if it's one we have identified and kept track of over the years.

If you were to give a young biologist one piece of advice, what would you tell him or her?
We are on the brink of new frontiers in science. The problems of extinction, pollution, and population growth will have to be addressed. In order for important changes to occur it will require teamwork and dedication using individuals with many different skills, including scientists, business people, developers, and others. To become an effective biologist, it is essential to gain the skills of communication and cooperation. It will also be important to gain a broad base of knowledge in fields other than pure science. It may be necessary to volunteer as a means of acquiring useful skills. The experience can be invaluable. Science has traditionally been a male-dominated field. However, just as in politics, women are making great inroads toward creating a better balance. As a woman, it is important to remember that while barriers may exist, they can be overcome through education of those around you regarding your abilities.

Orca Research in Puget Sound, Washington
by Ken Balcomb, Moclips Cetological Society, 1993

When we would see a pod of killer whales consisting of a male and four females and several offspring in 1963, our guess was that it was a harem bull (*male leader of the group*) and its mates and their calves. The truth of it is that one of those females is "mom" or even "grandmom" and the others are siblings. They stay in family kinship groups that are matrilined (*female genetic lines in a population*). In other words, the mother and her offspring stay together throughout their lifetime. Even the males stay with their mothers. The bull probably does not mate within that pod (*group of whales*) or matriline. It probably gets introduced to whales in other pods by mom and the mating is between matrilines rather than within. So if you see a pod of killer whales the leader of the group is the oldest female. It's kind of like elephants who are also matrilined. It's phenomenal!

I started this project in 1976 and immediately realized that we could recognize individual whales. This meant that we could study orcas over a long period of time and find out the number of calves each mother gives birth to, how many live to adulthood and how many die. Seventeen years later and this project is really starting to bear fruit in terms of how much we really know about killer whales.

Twenty years ago, no one knew how long orcas lived, how often they had calves, or when they matured. The information in books on killer whales was all wrong. In 1981, five years after we started the study, we were expecting the calves to be grown up. Well, we discovered that it took 14 years for an orca to mature. So the age of sexual maturity was a lot higher than expected. Then, based upon a lot of early photo work and published photographs in papers, lists of captures and so on, we have been able to put together information that suggests female survivors live to age 80 and males to age 50. The average life span is comparable to that of humans. That was a real surprise because the published literature said that they live 20 years or more. Since killer whales are at the top of the food chain, it makes sense that they are long-lived animals with low reproductive rates.

The maximum birth rate we have seen is one calf every three years. Gestation (*length of pregnancy*) is 17 months. On the average, an adult female will produce five calves in a lifetime and will not produce any calves after the age of 40. Females have a very long post-reproductive life which is probably of some social significance. Orca societies are polygamous (*a female will mate with more than one male and vice versa*).

The St. Lawrence Beluga Whales
Edited by Pierre Beland, St. Lawrence National Institute of Ecotoxicology.
Montreal, Quebec, Canada.

The beluga is a small white whale (up to 16 feet) that inhabits the arctic
regions of the world. However, there is one isolated population of belugas
in the St. Lawrence River, Quebec, Canada—almost 1000 miles outside of
the normal range of other beluga whales. The St. Lawrence River is part
of the largest drainage system in eastern North America and includes the
Great Lakes (Lake Ontario, Lake Erie, Lake Michigan, and others). There
are many industrial cities (Toronto, Detroit, Chicago, Cleveland, and
others) that border the Great Lakes and are responsible for contributing
to the water pollution in the lakes.

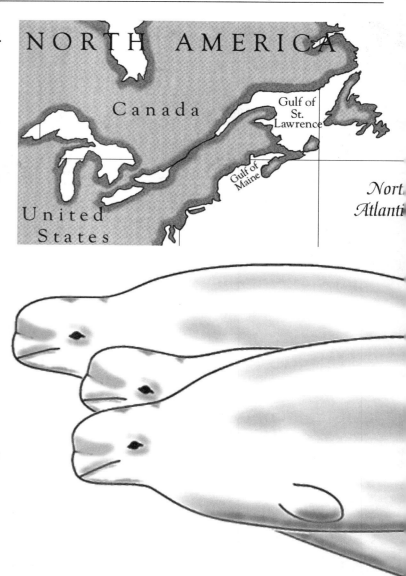

The beluga population in the St. Lawrence River was hunted by humans
for more than 200 years. Originally, they were hunted for their oil and
skins. In the 1930s, fishermen blamed the belugas for poor salmon and
cod catches. The Quebec fisheries authorized aerial bombing raids on the
whales and established a bounty of $15 per whale. Within a six year pe-
riod more than 2,000 whales were killed.

The original population was believed to be more than 5,000 whales. Yet
today, the population is thought to be as low as 450 to 500 animals. In
1979, a law was passed to protect the whales from being hunted. Today,
there is a more deadly killer that lurks silently in the waters of the St.
Lawrence. Since 1982, scientists Pierre Beland and Daniel Martineau of
the St. Lawrence National Institute of Ecotoxicology (*study of the effects of
pollution on animals*) have been studying the effects of water pollution on
beluga whales. They have examined more than 15 dead belugas a year
and discovered whales with tumors, bladder cancer, and open sores on
their bodies. The belugas of the St. Lawrence are indicators of the health
of the waters in that region. Belugas have high levels of deadly chemicals
in their bodies, including PCBs, DDT, lead, mercury, and the insecticide
Mirex. These are all deadly chemicals that are found in the waters of the
St. Lawrence. The industrial sewage outflows from companies that are on
the lakes and along the rivers have devastated the quality of the water.

Beland was able to track Mirex to a company that manufactured it on
Lake Ontario in the 1960s. Leakages of the chemical into the lake pro-

duced large-scale fish contamination and eventually led to the banning of Mirex in the 1970s.

Now more than 20 years after the banning of the chemical, eels that live in Lake Ontario are still contaminated with high levels of Mirex in their bodies. (The same is true for the chemical DDT.)

Belugas feed on large numbers of eels that migrate from Lake Ontario to the Gulf of St. Lawrence. The belugas, which are at the top of the food chain, are very susceptible to chemicals like Mirex that take generations to *break down*, since they get all of the contaminants that eels and other small fish have acquired in the polluted areas of the Great Lakes. Beland has found that the level of Mirex in the blubber of the belugas is ten times higher than that found in the eels.

The bladder cancer found in belugas probably comes from aluminum plants along the Saguenay River (which drains into the St. Lawrence). Workers at the plants had reported 130 cases of bladder cancer by 1990. Aluminum plant workers most likely to develop bladder cancer were exposed to extremely high levels of a chemical known as PAH. Belugas are known to have PAH in their bodies.

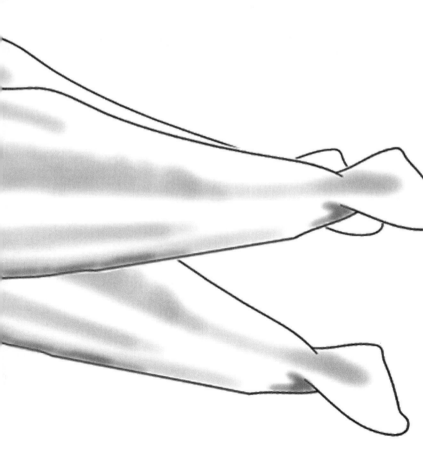

The future for the St. Lawrence belugas does not look too bright. Evidence shows beluga birthrates are low, only balancing the 20-30 deaths per year. Media articles about the belugas have raised the awareness of many citizens. Some of the industrial companies responsible for the pollution of the St. Lawrence have stepped forward to clean up their share of the disaster. Alcan Aluminum has given more than $100,000 for research on St. Lawrence belugas, while other companies have done little or have been forcibly closed down. The chemicals that have been dumped in the Great Lakes are extremely long-lived. If all dumping were stopped immediately, the chemicals would still persist in the environment for hundreds of years.

What is the lesson to be learned from the story of the St. Lawrence belugas? It is not a happy story, but a bitter pill to swallow. Humans have destroyed the water quality in this beautiful river. This is a legacy that will be felt by all of us long past the extinction of the St. Lawrence belugas.

Whale Watching vs. Whaling
Are whales worth more alive than they are dead?

From an interview with Erich Hoyt and excerpts from his article "Whale Watching Around the World," Whale and Dolphin Conservation Society, 1992.

The whale watching industry has grown tremendously in the past decade. It is beginning to rival the economic value of the whaling industry itself. In 1991, an estimated four million people went whale watching worldwide. In doing so more than $350,000,000 was spent (including travel, lodging, food, etc.) on whale watching. Off the east coast of the United States alone, more than 1.5 million people went whale watching in 1991. Whales are worth more alive than they are dead. You couldn't have said that five years ago, but you can say it today.

The educational value of whale watching is tremendous. Both schoolchildren and adults learn about whales and the marine environment. Many people come back from whale watching trips and develop a passion for protecting whales and the marine environment. Whale watching has also helped provide funds for whale research, and the boats have allowed many researchers to get out and do their work at sea.

In June 1992 the International Whaling Commission (IWC) met to reconsider whaling after a four-year moratorium. Norway and Iceland have chosen to resume whaling. (The whales are killed for human consumption.) Japan, too, wants to do whaling again. Yet these three countries now have active whale watching industries. Japan's whale watching began in 1988 and now has five whale watching ports. In 1991, there were more than 8,700 whale watchers and the industry brought in a total revenue of $4,000,000 (U.S.). Fishermen such as Mr. Tomohisa Nagaoka, a retired Antarctic whaler who is enthusiastic about whale watching, takes visitors on 13-passenger boats. Norway also started in 1988 and has the most successful whale watching operation in Europe. In 1991, whale watchers from 26 countries (mostly Norway and Sweden) came to look for sperm whales, minkes, and orcas. Iceland just began whale watching in 1991.

It is the minke that the whalers want to kill in northern Norway. Whaling may conflict with the whale watching industry in Norway as well as in other places. Is the conservation movement and support for whale watching in these whaling countries strong enough to stop whaling altogether? Whale watching is beginning to show that it might compete economically with whaling. If whaling continues, they will be wasting not only the lives of magnificent sea creatures, but an opportunity to educate people about the seas and sea life.

Erich Hoyt aboard
Japanese whale-watching ship

Will the Blue Whale Survive into the 21st Century?

The blue whale is the largest creature that has ever lived on our planet—larger than the greatest of dinosaurs and many times larger than an elephant. And yet many have predicted that this giant may become extinct by the year 2000. The blue whale's extinction, if it occurs, will be entirely at the hands of humans—specifically whalers. What a tremendous loss to our planet to not have the blue whale swimming in the ocean waters.

Blue whales were not a preferred whale to kill until the late 1800s. The whale was too fast for the wind-driven ships to catch, and it sank when it was killed. However, a Norwegian whaler named Sven Foyn began using a faster steam-driven ship that had a cannon-like harpoon gun mounted on the bow. When a whale was killed, a long tube was pushed into the body cavity and compressed air was pumped into it to keep it afloat.

The greatest destruction of blue whales occurred after 1900 when the whaling grounds of Antarctica were discovered. It is believed that most of the world's blue whale population lived in Antarctica. The development of the factory ship, a floating whale factory, in 1925 was the final nail in the blue whale's coffin. These ships could process large numbers of blue whales in the open sea. In 1931 alone 29,000 blue whales were killed in Antarctica. Conservationist Scott McVay once said about factory ship whaling, "Nothing is wasted except the whale itself."

The International Whaling Commission, a protective agency, knew that blue whale populations were low, but members could not agree that the whales needed full protection. For a time some members of the IWC believed that there was a separate subspecies of blue whale called the "pygmy blue whale" (probably two-to five-year-old whales) and that there were enough of this species of blue whale to continue killing them. So the killing went on for ten additional years until 1965, when even the so-called "pygmy blue whales" were so rare that the whalers could not find them. Finally the blue whale had protection, but was it too late?

Blue Whale photograph by James Cotton

In George Small's classic 1971 book *The Blue Whale,* he expresses mournful pessimism about the blue whale's chances for survival. "Are there any lonely members of that great species alive in all the North Atlantic? Yes, probably a few. If the animal does not become extinct in the Atlantic, it will be a miracle." He stated that there are so few blue whales that they may not be able to find mates in the open expanses of the ocean.

In the past 20 years, however, there have been a number of discoveries that lead to new hope about their survival. Yes, the population of blue whales is low. But various researchers have identified more than 250 blue whales in the Gulf of St. Lawrence, Quebec, Canada. Calves have been observed during the study. In the eastern tropical Pacific concentrations of blue whales and calves have been observed. This may indeed be the calving grounds of the North Pacific blue whale.

Researchers have learned more about blue whale vocalizations (*sounds*), too. They have discovered that blue whales may emit one of the most powerful sounds on Earth. This sound may travel hundreds of miles, allowing solitary blues to stay in communication with other blue whale pods. It is now believed that blue whales form pods that may disperse and spread out hundreds of miles.

Will the blue whale survive? View it with great hope and encouragement, but don't forget about the past slaughter of blue whales. All life on this planet is fragile. Even the giant blue whale could not survive the attack of uncaring humans. We humans must live with other species on this planet and not let greed and money interfere with the value of life.

Greenpeace and the Whale War

Greenpeace is one of the most famous environmental groups in the world. It first gained public attention in 1975 for tracking down Russian whaling ships and trying to halt the slaughter of whales. Its strategy was to maneuver a boat between the whale and the harpoon gunner. At one point a harpoon was actually fired over the heads of the protesters and killed a young sperm whale. Greenpeace's work received a lot of public attention and helped develop awareness about whales.

When laws banned whaling from 1978 to the early 1980s, pirate whalers appeared who wouldn't comply with these laws. Greenpeace launched an all-out fight against them. One pirate ship was rammed, three others were sunk by bombs (Greenpeace does not take responsibility for the bombings), and another was sunk when the weight of a recently killed fin whale caused the heavily-laden ship to list (*lean over*) too far in high seas.

In 1985, the Greenpeace ship *Rainbow Warrior* was sunk when it was bombed in a New Zealand harbor by French commandos. The *Rainbow Warrior* was in position to protest French nuclear testing in the Pacific Ocean.

In 1986, a worldwide ban on whaling was called for by the International Whaling Commission. At this time other radical conservation groups joined the battle and actually did more harm than good. Negative public reaction to their tactics set the conservation movement's efforts back in many ways.

Despite the ban in 1986, Iceland continued to hunt whales. *Sea Shepard*, a radical conservation group, came to Iceland, sunk two whaling ships, and destroyed the only whaling station. Many Icelandic conservationists believe that the destruction of the whaling station set back hopes for ending whaling a good ten years. The Icelandic people were so outraged by the action of *Sea Shepard* that there was a huge backlash against the whale conservation cause.

The warlike tactics of Greenpeace and other groups in the name of conservation are highly questionable. However, Greenpeace's work has caused a number of positive changes that have helped protect whales and life on our planet.

The Children's Save the Whale Campaign

Most school-age children think of themselves as powerless to create change in the world around them. Children hear about pollution and animals becoming extinct, but they are not sure what to do.

In the early 1970s, there were no laws that protected whales. Through public awareness campaigns, schoolchildren saw the mass destruction of whales and joined together to write millions of letters to Congress and the President. They also educated their parents about the wonders of whales. At that time, whales were viewed more as giant hamburgers swimming in our seas. The sensitive and caring letters from five-to twelve-year-olds had a huge impact on Congress and the President. The children were effective because they had the ability to express the truth in a heartfelt way.

Their work paid off. In 1972, Congress passed the Marine Mammal Protection Act which protected whales in United States waters. But whales were still dying in other parts of the world. The movement spread to Canada, Australia, and other countries. Slowly whaling came to an end. In 1986, a complete ban on whaling was declared in the world (Japan, Norway, and Iceland do not adhere to the ban and still kill whales).

The real lesson from this event is that children can create change in their world. Let's say there is a park in your town where you and your friends play. City officials decide they want to put in a golf course where your park is. If you believe in preserving your park, fight for it! Go to the city council meetings and voice your opinion, write your local newspaper, get your class and school involved in the fight.

Captive Orcas

From an interview with Erich Hoyt and excerpts from his report, *The Performing Orca —Why the Show Must Stop.*

Overview

For my report, I visited most of the 17 aquariums where killer whales are being kept and talked to trainers and owners. Having worked with orcas in the wild, I have always had mixed feelings about keeping them in captivity.

Sea World Inc. is the main exhibitor of orcas in the world. The "Shamu" caricature of an orca, the sea panda that loves to be kissed and mischievously splashes you, is always front and center. One "educational" message promoted by Sea World is what I call the "Shamu lie." Since the mid-1960s, Sea World has used the same names for its performing orcas. One might assume these animals were the same few that Sea World started with 30 years ago. The truth is that there have been nearly 40 orcas displayed at all four Sea World parks, most of them with the name "Shamu."

Do Killer Whales Need Much Space?

If marine parks are going to keep captive orcas, I think we have to look at what their real needs might be. Orcas travel 75 to 100 miles a day in the wild.

In captivity, orcas are kept in bare, featureless tanks, the largest of which are only approximately five million cubic gallons. Compared to this tank, the size of just the resting and playing areas for typical wild orcas is at least 6,000 times larger.

Accidents Caused by Captive Orcas

In 1990, a young female trainer was killed by three orcas at Sealand in Victoria, British Columbia. The three whales had been kept in a metal holding pool that was scarcely larger than their body length (26-foot diameter). They had to stay in the tank for 15 hours a day, except when they were performing. If they didn't return to the holding tank after performing, trainers would withhold 1/3 of their daily food. Sealand officials called the death a tragic accident. However, given the strained living conditions of the whales, it is not surprising that a tragedy happened.

There have been dozens of accidents and near-deaths of trainers. Is it the fault of the training programs and the inexperience of the trainers? Or do the orcas become bored and their behavior distorted, unpredictable, and dangerous after long periods in captivity? Probably it's a combination of all these factors.

Social Needs of Orcas

A third of the world's orca aquariums have only one orca. This is inexcusable, since orcas are very social mammals that live in pods of up to 50 animals. Wild orcas, even males, stay in the same pod with their mothers their whole lives. In many of the aquariums orcas from different pods are housed together. The largest number of orcas kept at one aquarium is five or six, less than the typical pod size.

Premature Deaths of Killer Whales

We know wild male orcas live an average of 29 years and females an average of 50 years. (This knowledge comes from widely accepted scientific studies based on the life histories of the northwest coast orcas.) Orcas have only been kept captive since 1961, which is barely enough time for a male to live to an average life span and not enough time for a female. The longest an orca has lived in captivity is 23 years (as of December 1992). The record-holder is one female who is still alive, named "Corky." Only one male, an individual named "Orky," lived to the average age for a wild orca. He died at about age 30. To date, captive orcas are living fewer years than those in the wild.

Captive Breeding Program

Since 1985, Sea World has had considerable success in the captive breeding of orcas (six successful births in seven years). It has put millions of dollars into this program. Yet, in some cases, the calves are taken from their mothers at an age of less than one year and moved between the other Sea World parks at opposite ends of the country. The removal of calves from their mothers is another example of how the social needs of the animals are being ignored. Is such treatment having an impact on the parents of the calves? Most have died within a relatively short time after fathering or mothering calves. Over half the mothers and all but one of the fathers have died.

Performing orcas are big business. In some cases a million dollars may change hands during a sale. Certainly, quite a few have sold within the range of $100,000 to $500,000. In the future, orcas are going to be worth more since it is so hard to import them. The U.S. aquariums haven't been able to obtain any permits to import orcas from the wild for the last couple of years. They are forced to buy orcas from other aquariums. The situation is so desperate that Sea World imported from Sealand in Canada the orcas that killed their trainer (despite protests from Sea World's own trainers). Sea World wouldn't need to keep buying more orcas if its animals weren't dying prematurely.

Marine Zoological Parks: The Public Benefit
Dr. Dan O'Dell, research biologist, Sea World

Overview
For most people who visit marine life parks, including Sea World, it is the only opportunity they have to see dolphins or killer whales firsthand. Finding yourself nose-to-nose with a killer whale or seeing a dolphin leap gracefully from the water is a memorable experience; one that leaves a lasting impression. Over the years, we've discovered our visitors come away with a newfound respect for marine mammals and a desire to learn more about the marine environment and how to protect it.

This focus on education, conservation, and research is key to what we do at Sea World. For example, each year more than 600,000 students take part in our in-park marine science programs and millions more participate nationwide in our satellite education broadcasts.

Research
Some knowledge of killer whale biology comes from research done at Sea World. We are able to watch the animals 24 hours a day, every day of the year. This has helped us learn a tremendous amount about them over a relatively short period of time.

For example, we know a lot about the growth rate of killer whale calves. The animals are trained to position themselves so we can weigh and measure them. They also present their tail flukes so that we may take blood samples. Observations such as these are not possible for researchers studying killer whales in the wild.

The most recent scientific studies suggest that a killer whale's life span is between 25 and 35 years regardless of where it lives. It's important to remember field researchers have been studying killer whales for only 20 years. It's pure speculation when they conclude these animals may live to a maximum of 50 to 60 years.

Another area in which we've made great strides is in the breeding of killer whales. Sea World now has the world's most successful breeding program, with nine healthy calves born since 1985. In 1993, we observed the birth of the world's first second-generation killer whale at Sea World of Texas, whose mother was also born at Sea World.

We are extremely proud of our breeding program. Biologists consider breeding a clear indicator of an animal's ability to thrive in its environment. Our reproduc-

tive successes are an important indicator that the killer whales are provided with a habitat that has all of the key components. The same is true for our bottlenose dolphins. More than half of Sea World's dolphins, including many second generation ones, were born at our parks.

Quality Care of Killer Whales

We take many steps to ensure the health and well-being of all of our animals, including the killer whales. Sea World's staff includes full-time veterinarians, animal care specialists, and trainers, many of whom have dedicated their careers to caring for these animals.

Sea World's facilities are the biggest of their kind in the world, far exceeding standards set by the U.S. government. Our killer whales live in habitats where the water quality and temperature are carefully monitored and controlled. Unlike killer whales in the oceans, those at Sea World are not forced to contend with dangers such as shortages of food, parasites, and threats from humans. In addition, our veterinarians perform regular checkups during which they evaluate the animal's health. At Sea World, the killer whales receive a balanced, nutritious diet, and we make sure their day includes plenty of exercise.

Conservation

Killer whales are not endangered; however, knowledge we gain from working with animals that are not endangered helps us in saving species that are endangered. Sea World rescues and rehabilitates many endangered marine animals, including the Florida manatee. There are less than 2,000 of these unusual-looking creatures left in Florida. Since 1977, we have treated more than 100 sick, orphaned, and injured manatees. Visitors to Sea World of Florida now have a rare chance to observe these manatees in a new habitat. The idea behind this attraction is to show people that manatees are an important part of the aquatic ecosystem in Florida, and to let people know what they can do to help. Between our California and Florida parks, we rescue every year hundreds of animals such as sea lions, seals, birds, and others. In fact, in just the last two years, Sea World has rescued, rehabilitated, and returned to the wild more marine mammals than have been collected by Sea World during our 28-year history.

Conclusion

We don't know all there is to know about killer whales, but Sea World's staff is making important contributions. Neither lab nor field studies alone can provide all of the answers. Investigators in both areas must continue to work together. Sea World's work with killer whales is part of our overall commitment to education, conservation, and research. By offering the public an opportunity to see animals up close, we help inspire concern not only for them but also for their habitats. This, in turn, creates a base of public support needed to protect all of the world's ecosystems.

Dan O'Dell

The 1987-88 Dolphin Die-Off on the U.S. East Coast

During the summer of 1987, two or three dolphins a week began washing up on the crowded beaches of the New Jersey coast. Many had lesions (*sores*) on their bodies, and their lungs were congested with fluids. Not only were scientists alarmed, but all of the beach-goers were feeling that there was something wrong in the coastal waters. Medical wastes began showing up on the beach, including syringes and intravenous bags. Swimmers complained of sickness. The headlines of newspapers read, "Don't Go Near the Water." As the summer wore on, more and more dolphins continued to die as far south as Florida. Tests from the health department showed that the water was safe for swimmers, but why were so many dolphins dying?

The National Marine Fisheries Service authorized an investigation. Dr. Joseph Geraci, a specialist in marine mammals, headed the project. The study was coordinated with several laboratories along the Atlantic coast. The scientists were really trying to find a particular cause of the deaths. This was extremely difficult since most dolphins already had a number of environmental contaminants stored in their bodies. Even today it is still not known what the life-threatening toxic levels are for various contaminants in most whales and dolphins.

One contaminant the scientists found in the dead dolphins was PCBs (polychlorinated-biphenols). PCBs—once used in refrigeration and insulation—have been banned in the United States since 1979, but it is the type of chemical that persists in the environment for many years. PCBs damage reproductive systems and can stop animals from bearing young. PCBs also suppress the immune system, which makes animals more susceptible to diseases.

By March 1988, more than 740 dolphins had died. Almost half of the entire near shore population of bottlenose dolphins that lived along the east coast of the U.S. was dead. The scientists turned up evidence that the dolphins had died from *red tide*.

[Red tide is not a tide at all. It is caused by naturally-occurring microscopic organisms called "dinoflagellates." They are a type of phytoplankton and under special environmental conditions will produce toxins that affect other animals in the food chain. Along sea coasts, most humans are aware of periodic shellfish poisoning. When a red tide occurs, people can die from eating contaminated shellfish, such as clams and mussels.]

The theory was that fish had picked up the red tide toxin in the Gulf of Mexico. The fish travelled north to the east coast of the U.S., where the dolphins began feeding on them. Addressing a press conference on the problem, Dr. Geraci said that the bottlenose dolphins had died of poisoning from eating the fish carrying the red tide toxin. One journalist asked, "You mean pollution had nothing to do with the dolphin deaths?" "Nothing!" Geraci replied.

Many other researchers and environmentalists found Geraci's explanation too simple. How could Geraci have ignored the fact that he had found extraordinarily high levels of PCBs in the livers of many of the dolphins? What about all of the respiratory problems that Geraci had found? He himself had noted that the problems were like those contracted from inhaling a toxic gas. Further investigations on the problem were held and the scientists finally agreed that pollution was probably part of the problem.

Conclusion

Are we finally seeing the effects from the polluting of our seas? Whales and dolphins are visible monitors of the health of our oceans. The 1987 die-off of half the coastal population of bottlenose dolphins was an ominous warning that pollution must stop. Since 1987, there have been some changes. There is more awareness about marine pollution and coastal dumping of toxic materials than ever before.

But is enough being done to stop the pollution of our oceans? Many would argue that much more needs to be done before it is too late.

Up Close and Personal with a Whale Biologist
Ken Balcomb

How did you get hooked on whale research?
After finishing college, I heard about a whale research expedition and hired on as a dishwasher. Later on, the chief scientist saw my enthusiasm and hired me as a biologist for other research expeditions. We went off the coast of Mexico, and in those years you could run into thousands and thousands of spinner, spotted, and common dolphins. We also saw the occasional blue and humpback whale. Roughly 10 to 15 times a day we would have sightings of whales and dolphins and it was always exciting.

What are the most exciting observations that you have made?
One of the real thrilling things for anyone going into a scientific career is to discover a new species or a "lost species." I had that experience in 1966. I was on a cruise in an area that was relatively "dead" and where very few other biologists had visited. We were on the equator at 165° W, and I saw a fairly large school of dolphins. In my mind, I went through every species they might be and I knew that I had never seen them before. I took some photos of the dolphin school and showed them to other dolphin experts, and no one could identify them. After a lot of sleuthing around, we concluded that they were *Lagenodelphis hosei*, Fraser's dolphin, described in 1895 by a scientist from a single specimen washed up on a beach in Borneo. I had rediscovered a "lost" species and was the first scientist to ever see this type of dolphin alive. Seven years later, another scientist working for the tuna-porpoise project came up with a couple of specimens and they matched my photos exactly.

That same day, I ran into about 25 large beaked whales. They were curious about us and swam right around the boat. I got some incredible photos of the whales. I deduced by comparing the photographs with measurements taken from the skulls of whales at a museum that these were southern bottlenose whales. This type of whale had never been seen near the equator. In fact, its range was thought to be from Australia south to Antarctica.

Ken Balcomb
Photo courtesy of Barbara Solberg

It must be like going through a new door making a discovery like that. Can you describe what it feels like?

It is thrilling! The neat thing about it is there are more "doors" out there to go through. Like the beaked whale, *Mesoplodon peruviana* is a new species that was just described in Peru from a washed up specimen. Just last winter we photographed some bizarre beaked whales off the Bahamas. Beaked whales are my fancy because they are so unknown. They are the most unknown of the unknown.

What can you say about the effects of the oil spill on the whales that live in Prince William Sound?

Craig Matkin, a commercial fisherman who has had some government contracts studying whale populations in Prince William Sound, reports there were about 180 killer whale residents and 103 other whales. Within a week of the spill, seven resident killer whales were missing. When we say "missing" we knew that they were dead because of the tight social structure of killer whales. A total of 27 are now dead and I don't think we are through. I think the food chain effects are going to be felt for 20 to 40 years. I do know that the oil is in the pebbles and rocks in the benthic system (*on the bottom*) anywhere from six inches to two to three feet down. It's just a huge layer of oil underneath and I think that will keep turning up in the food chain, especially in the bottom level.

What goals or dreams do you have for the next 20 years?

Before I quit this business or life, I've got to get some of this information out to the public because there is no one around who has had some of these experiences. In 1984, we wrote *The World's Whales*, a Smithsonian book. I would like to see the book redone because the level of knowledge on cetaceans (*whales, dolphins, and porpoises*) has jumped considerably. Also, I am still looking for a whale I photographed that first winter in 1966. I got some pictures of humpbacks in Mexico, and I want to find one of those right now. It's like Ahab, I haven't found that whale but I'm still looking.

Whale Dreams and Visions

Orca Dreams
by Erich Hoyt

Erich Hoyt spent ten summers (in the 1970s and 1980s) living among orcas off Vancouver Island, Canada. His group of researchers grew close to one particular pod of whales. They were with the whales day in and day out, and were often awakened by them three to four times a night as the whales swam by their camp. One of the beloved elders of the pod was an old female named Stubbs, so called because of her stubby, mangled dorsal fin. She had probably once had a boating accident, a too-close encounter with a boat propeller. For several days, the researchers had not seen Stubbs with the rest of the pod and were concerned about her disappearance. There seemed a hole in their days...something missing. An unexpected dream helped fill that hole, as dreams often do.

We are on the beach watching Stubbs' full pod, except for Stubbs, navigate a narrow passage. I remember walking into the water, blind at first, trying to catch some whale's eye. It was the way one walks into a crowd, looking for a sign of welcome.

I see this cow. Our eyes meet. We touch. The experience of touching seems to make all words unnecessary. Whales and people are standing around now, as if at a party. I make my way over to Sturdy (one of the males in the pod). Dark, formidable, massive, Sturdy is yet friendly.

"You know the whale we call Stubbs?" I ask, hesitantly. "What is your name for her?"
Sturdy smiles. "Oh yes, she is Smirilak."
"Where is she?" I ask.." Why isn't she with you?"
Sturdy points down and over toward the side of the narrow passage

to the beach. I don't understand the gesture.
"She died?"
Sturdy only nods.
I look down, feeling upset. Sturdy is puzzled at my reaction. It makes no sense to him that I should feel badly about her death. He shrugs. "She is dead, that's all."
I say nothing but I am sad, thinking of Stubbs' death. Yet I am also relieved to know. Sturdy makes it easier to accept.

Seeing the whales, talking with them, I feel alive, completely aware at this moment. I tell myself this is really happening; it is not a dream. Between men and whales, all things suddenly seem possible.

With permission from *Orca: The Whale Called Killer* by Erich Hoyt

A Dolphin on the Beach
by Roger Payne

I was working in a laboratory at Tufts University one March night during a sleet storm when I heard through the local radio news that a dead whale had washed ashore on Revere Beach. I wanted to see it so I drove out there. The sleet had turned to rain when I reached the place. Many people had come to see the whale earlier but there were only a few on the beach when I arrived and by the time I reached the place where the whale lay, the beach was deserted.

It was a small whale, a porpoise about eight feet long with lovely subtle curves glistening in the cold rain. It had been mutilated. Someone had hacked off its flukes for a souvenir. Two other people had carved their initials deeply into its side, and someone else had stuck a cigar butt in its blowhole. I removed the cigar and stood there for a long time with feelings I cannot describe. Everybody has some such experience that affects him or her for life, probably several. That night was one of mine.

At some point my flashlight went out, but as the tide came in I could periodically see the graceful outline of the whale against the white foam cast by the waves. Although it is more typical than not of what happens to whales when they encounter people, that experience was somehow the last straw, and I decided to use the first possible opportunity to learn enough about whales so I might have some effect on their fate.

A Swim with a Blue Whale
by Richard Sears
Sea of Cortez, Baja California, March 1986

I remember one day in the Sea of Cortez, a blue whale that we were observing stopped dead in the water. You could see the blue-green hue of the animal as it "logged" just below the surface. I had to see what the whale looked like underwater. This was my chance. We stopped the boat and a couple of us jumped in with masks and so on. I went swimming over to it. The whale was probably 30 meters away from me, but the visibility was only 10 meters at best. As I approached the whale, my heart was pounding. I knew that it was big. Somehow my curiosity made me brave. As I swam toward the whale I could see a green hue in the water. It got lighter and lighter as I swam closer and all of a sudden there was a HUGE WHALE! I swam in on its right side. In front of me was a huge animal draped in the water, tail to the left and the head to the right. I came within five feet of it and took a few pictures. I felt small and insignificant. My heart was really pounding, from the thrill, excitement, and fear of having this beast in front of me. I swam toward the head, and it glided down, slowly, out of sight. Then I was by myself, and I started thinking about sharks and swam like crazy to get back to the boat.

Adopt-A-Whale

One way that you can support whale research is to "adopt" a whale. Below I have included the Adopt-A-Whale programs of several of the researchers who contributed to this book. The money you contribute will go directly to research on the whales. Your contributions will allow scientists to continue their important work. In most cases, you will receive a 4" x 6" photo of the animal; a certificate; a general information sheet about that particular species; a complete sighting history; and information on research being presently conducted.

Right Whale Adoptions
East Coast Ecosystems Right Whale Adoption Program
P.O. Box 31
Westport, Nova Scotia, Canada
BPV 1HO
(902) 839-2962
Moira Brown belongs to this research group. She contributed an "Up Close and Personal" interview (page 54).

North Atlantic Right Whale Project
New England Aquarium
Central Wharf
Boston, MA 02110-3399
(617) 973-6582
Amy Knowlton belongs to this research group and contributed an "Up Close and Personal" interview (page 106) and the information for the activity "Can the North Atlantic Right Whale Survive the Next 50 Years?" (page 104).

Blue Whale
Mingan Island Cetacean Study
285 Green
St. Lambert, Quebec J4P1T3
Canada
Richard Sears is the leader of this research group and contributed
an "Up Close and Personal" Interview (page 88) and "A Swim with a
Blue Whale" (page 129).

Fin Whale
Allied Whale
College of the Atlantic
105 Eden St.
Bar Harbor, ME 04609
(207) 288-5644
Steve Katona was the founder of Allied Whale. He contributed an
"Up Close and Personal" interview (page 84). He also contributed
data for the migration studies of the North Atlantic humpback
whale (page 70) and the "Whale Tails" activity (page 74).

Killer Whale
Protect A Pod
P.O. Box 1577
Friday Harbor, WA 98250
Ken Balcomb contributed an "Up Close and Personal" interview
(page 124). He also contributed the article entitled "Orca Research
in Puget Sound, Washington" (page 108).

Bibliography

From Ocean to Land and Back

Balcomb, Kenneth. Whales of Hawaii. Marine Mammal Fund, 1987.

Evans, Peter. The Natural History of Whales and Dolphins. New York: Facts on File Inc., 1987.

Hoyt, Erich. Meeting the Whales. Firefly/Camden House, 1991.

Leatherwood, Steve. Whales, Dolphins, and Porpoises of the Eastern North Pacific. NOAA Technical Report NMFS Circular 444, 1982.

Katona, Steven et al. A Field Guide to the Whales, Porpoises and Seas of the Gulf of Maine and Eastern Canada. Scribners, 1983.

McAuliffe, Kathleen. Sea Frontiers. Vol. 40 No. 1 Jan/ Feb 1994 pp. 22-34.

Martin, Anthony R. Whales and Dolphins. Portland House, 1990.

Minasian, Stanley, Kenneth Balcomb and Larry Foster. The World's Whales. Washington D.C., Smithsonian Books, 1984.

Slijper, E. J.. Whales. Cornell University Press, 1979.

Trefil, James. Discover Magazine. May 1991, pp. 44-48.

Living The Life of a Whale

Andersen, Harald. Biology of Marine Mammals. Academic Press, 1969.

Cousteau, Jacques. Whales. Harry Abrams, Inc. New York, 1988. ("How whales feed.")

Gordon, David and Alan Baldridge. *Gray Whales*. Monterey Bay Aquarium, 1991. ("How whales feed.")

Slijper, E. J. Whales. Cornell University Press, 1979. ("How whales feed.")

Mitchell, Edward Dr., Larry Wade. Fisheries Research Board of Canada. Unpublished data, 1973. ("How Long Does a Whale Dive?")

Whale Research

Hoyt, Erich. Seasons of the Whale. Chelsea Green Publishing Company, 1990.

Leatherwood, S. Whales, Dolphins, and Porpoises of the Eastern North Pacific. US Dept. of Commerce, NOAA Technical Report NMFS Circular 444, July 1982. ("Whale Migration")

Katona, Steve. Allied Whale, College of the Atlantic, personal communication. Contributed data for "Whale Tails" and "Migration of the Great Whales," 1994.

Mitchell, Edward Dr., Larry Wade. Fisheries Research Board of Canada. Unpublished data, 1973. ("How Fast Does a Blue Whale Travel?")

Whaling and Conservation

Braham, Howard. National Marine Fisheries Service, Seattle, Washington. Unpublished data, 1993. ("Worldwide Estimates of Whale Populations")

Cobblestone Magazine. Whaling in America. Volume 5, Number 4. 1984.

Day, David. The Whale War. Sierra Club Books, 1987.

Dietz, Tim. Whales and Man. Yankee Publishing, 1987.

Ellis, Richard. Men and Whales. Alfred A. Knopf, 1991.

Knowlton, Amy. New England Aquarium, personal communication. (Contributed data for "Can the North Atlantic Right Whale Survive the Next 50 Years?"), 1993.

Mowat, Farley. Sea of Slaughter. Bantam Books, 1984.

Small, George. The Blue Whale. Columbia University Press, 1971.

Resources

Video

Beyond Belief—Humpback Whales
Includes bubble cloud feeding behavior, breaching, and close approaches.
1988; 50 minutes; $24.95. Cetacean Video: (1-800) 942-5390

The Great Whales
This is a historic documentary that includes footage of the "friendly" gray whales, the history of whaling, and Greenpeace conservation efforts.
1976; 60 minutes. National Geographic: (1-800) 368-2728; order no. G50514

In the Company of Whales
This excellent whale documentary is narrated by whale biologist Roger Payne (see pages 97 and 128). There is some footage on sperm whales, southern right whales, and dolphins.
1992; 90 minutes. Discovery Video Library: (1-800) 752-9073; order no. 23272

Killer Whales—Wolves of the Sea
1993; 60 minutes. National Geographic: (1-800) 368-2728; order no. G51555

Watching the Whales
This is an excellent video that has footage of blue whales, orcas, and other whales. It is not narrated, but the names of the whales are given.
1985; 30 minutes; $19.95. Marine Mammal Fund: (1-415) 775-4636

Whales!
This video has some excellent footage of right whales, whaling, and an orca attack on a blue whale.
1987; 60 minutes; $14.98. Audubon Video Series: (1-800) 326-1977; Live Home Video Order no. 15349

Wonderful Whales, Vol. 1
This video includes footage of humpback whale favorites: Salt, Olympia, Cat's Paw, and Ivory. It also includes footage of fin whales, pilot, and sperm whales.
1991; 30 minutes; $19.95. Cetacean Video: (1-800) 942-5390

Answer Pages

Page 9: Drawing a Whale

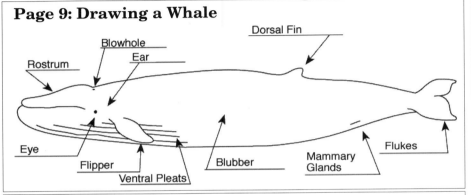

Rostrum
Blowhole
Ear
Dorsal Fin
Eye
Flipper
Ventral Pleats
Blubber
Mammary Glands
Flukes

Pages 14-15 Whale and Dolphin Key

A. Total Length: 49.5 ft.
Species: Right Whale

B. Total Length: 47 ft.
Species: Humpback

C. Total Length: 15 ft.
Species: Narwhal

D. Total Length: 90 ft.
Species: Blue Whale

E. Total Length: 26 ft.
Species: Orca

F. Total Length: 72 ft.
Species: Fin Whale

G. Total Length: 17 ft.
Species: Pilot Whale

H. Total Length: 14 ft.
Species: Beaked Whale

I. Total Length: 46 ft.
Species: Gray Whale

J. Total Length: 6 ft.
Species: Dolphin

K. Total Length: 6 ft.
Species: Porpoise

L. Total Length: 26 ft.
Species: Minke Whale

M. Total Length: 54 ft.
Species: Sperm Whale

N. Total Length: 14 ft.
Species: Beluga

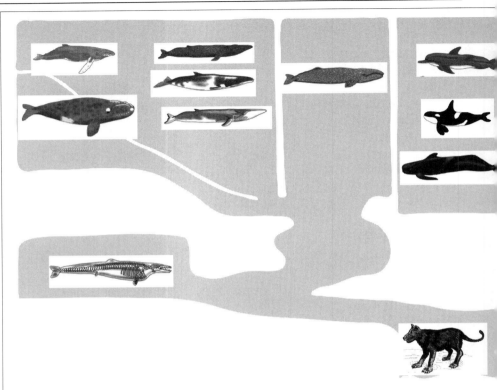

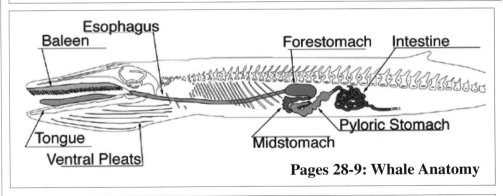

Esophagus
Baleen
Forestomach
Intestine
Tongue
Ventral Pleats
Midstomach
Pyloric Stomach

Pages 28-9: Whale Anatomy

Pages 30-1: 1. Wolves of the Sea; 2. Skim Feeders; 3. Suckers; 4. Bubble Cloud Feeders; 5. Grabbers; 6. Lunge Feeders; 7. Deep Divers

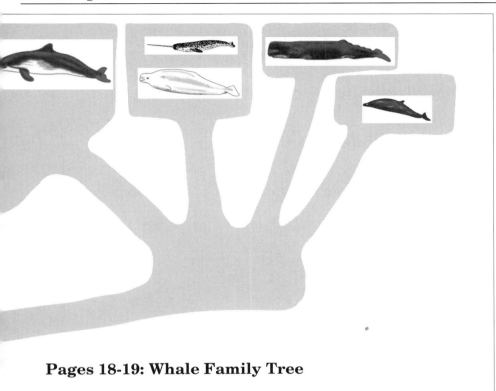

Pages 18-19: Whale Family Tree

Splash
Guard   Blowhole

Trachea
        Lungs   Ribs

Pages 46-7: Whale Respiration Anatomy

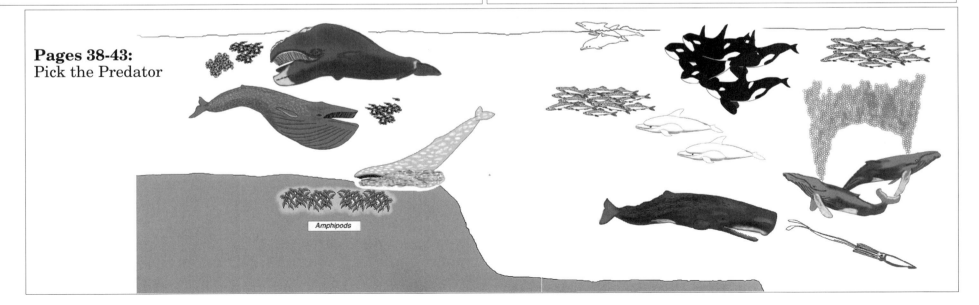

Pages 38-43:
Pick the Predator

Amphipods

P. 48: How Long Does a Whale Dive?

Minke Whale: 3.6 minutes
Blue Whale: ~ 11 minutes
Sperm Whale: ~ 58 minutes
Bottlenose Whale: ~ 36 minutes
Bottlenose dolphin: ~ 3 minutes

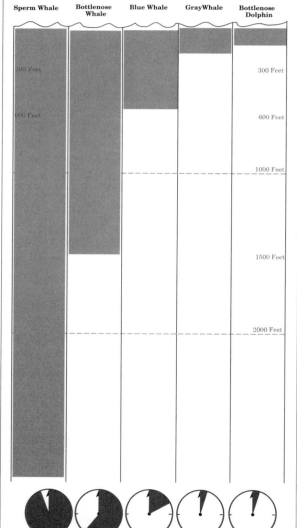

Pages 60-61: A Day With a Blue Whale

Daytime Observations: avg. no. of spouts: 10.1; avg. dive time: 11 min. Fluke-ups: 100%
Evening Observations: avg. no. of spouts: 1.6; avg. dive time: 1.4 min. Fluke-ups: 0%
Hypothesis: Food closer to surface at night, shorter dives possible, no fluke-ups because whale is making shallow dives. During the day, whale dives longer to find food in deeper water.

Pages 62: How Fast Does a Blue Whale Travel?

Location	Time	Distance	Speed
Base Camp to Pilot Station	.5 hrs. (30 min.)	2 miles	4 mph
Pilot Station to Ferry	.83 hrs. (50 min.)	3 miles	3.6 mph
Ferry to Au Rocher	1 hrs.	3.5 miles	3.5 mph
Totals:	2.33 hrs. (2:20)	8.5 miles	3.6 mph average

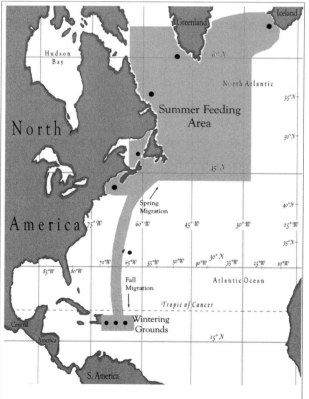

Page 71: N. Atlantic Humpback Whale

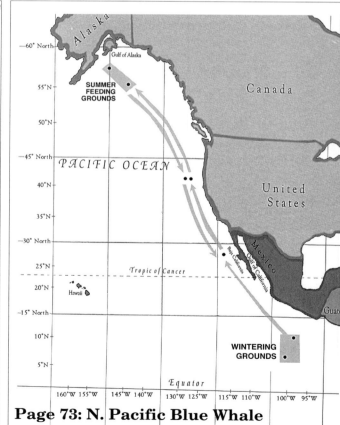

Page 73: N. Pacific Blue Whale

Pages 76-7: Whale Tail Activity

Whale Sighting Log	Added Information	Picture No.(MATCHES)
0054	8/86, Gulf of Maine	12
	11/86, Gulf of Maine	9
0153– Silver	7/90, Gulf of Maine with calf	1
	6/91, Gulf of Maine, found dead	14
4040	3/82, Dom. Republic, breeding grounds	3
	8/83, Greenland, feeding grounds	11

Question 1: The whale was female; she returned to the same area, had a calf every 2-3 years. Handicapped whales can survive in the wild.

Question 2: Every 2-3 years.

Question 3: They return to the same area.

Question 4: They share a common breeding ground, but visit different feeding grounds.

Pages 92-3 World-wide Estimates of Whale Populations

N. Atlantic Right Whale: 3 %
N. Pacific Bowhead Whale: 54%
N. Atlantic Blue Whale: 33 %

N. Pacific Gray Whale: 100%
N. Atlantic Humpback: 55%
N. Pacific Blue Whale: 41 %
Fin Whale(worldwide): 26 %

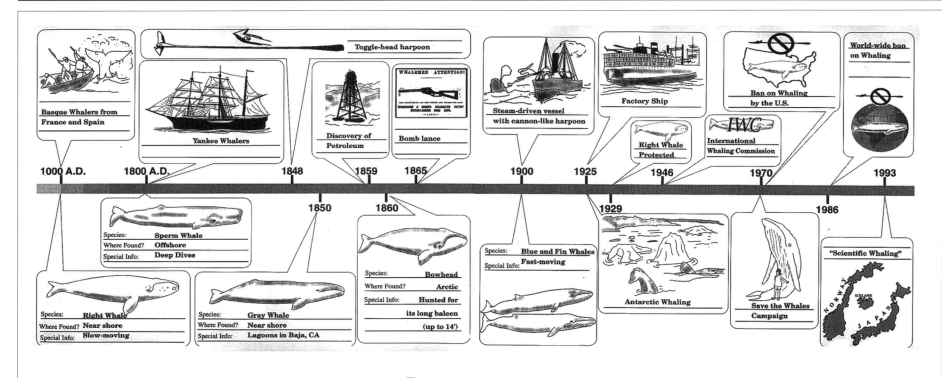

Pages 98-9:
Whale History
Time Line

Pages 100-1: Why Were Whales Hunted?

1. Sperm Oil:	$24,000
Whale Oil:	$37,152
Baleen:	$ 5,270
Total	$ 66,422

2. $66,422 x 20 = $ 1,328,440

3. Owner share	1843	$44,503
	1995	$890,055
4.Captain's share	1843	$ 8,303
	1995	$166,055
5. Seaman's share	1843	$443
	1995	$8,856

Pages 102-3 Whale Baleen and Women's Corsets

1. 1,661 whales
2. $ 682 (in 1850)
3. $ 1,132,740
4. $ 11,000 (in 1900)
5. $ 1,100 (in 1909)

Pages 104-5: Can the North Atlantic Right Whale Survive the Next 50 Years?

Year 2	Whales from calving	+12
	Whales from natural causes	-3
	Whales from entanglements and ships	-6
	Population size	**310**

Year 3	Whale Population Size: **310 Whales**	
	Whales from calving	+19
	Whales from natural causes	-3
	Population size	**326**

Year 4	Whale Population Size: **326 Whales**	
	Whales from calving	+16
	Whales from natural causes	-3
	Whales from oil spill	-33

Population size at the end of the four years: **306**

Question 1: The population barely increased.
Question 2: The conservation measures helped improve the growth of the population.
Question 3: Severe, negative effects on population size.

Up Close and Personal with the Author

The process of doing this book has been as meaningful as seeing it completed. This process began more than 20 years ago. I was a young whale biologist and determined to make my mark on the world. After several years of being on ships and in isolated places I started feeling a hollow spot in my heart that would not go away. I wanted the warmth of a family surrounding me. So I left the sea and went inland to Minnesota. My loving wife Carol and I have been blessed with three beautiful children, Laurel, Alli, and Aaron.

Over a decade ago, I started yearning for the sea again. I connected with scientists who were still studying whales. I wanted my students to develop a connection with the oceans and whales, so I started writing classroom activities. I love teaching and I love writing. For many years, I wrote an hour a day after school. It was a special time that I always looked forward to (even after a hard day). In completing this book, I had to find the best parts of myself. I have brought them to the world for all to see.

Working with the scientists on this book has brought me closer to the whales. These are people who love the ocean and the Earth. They are people who are dedicated to the protection of the whales and to improving their habitat. It is my hope that this book will bring YOU closer to whales too.!

Larry Wade
March 1995
Minnetonka, MN

Whales in the Classroom
Teacher Workshops and Curriculum Development

Author Larry Wade is available to contract with your college, school district, museum, or aquarium to perform any or all of the following services:

• Teacher Workshops

For teachers using the text *Whales in the Classroom Presents: Oceanography* and *Whales in the Classroom Presents: Getting to Know the Whales.*

• Week-long Graduate Level Education Course

Inland Whale Watching: This thematic course will show teachers how to incorporate art, geography, math, physical education, marine science, creative writing, and debate into their marine science and whale units.

• Curriculum Development

Do you need some fresh ideas on a curriculum topic that you are writing? Since 1985, Mr. Wade has developed interdisciplinary curricula on many natural science topics: marine science, mammals, birds, pond ecology, worms, deer, snakes, schoolyard nature areas, monarch butterflies, forest ecology, insects, and raptors.

Please contact the author through: **Singing Rock Press**
P.O. Box 1274
Minnetonka, MN 55345
Phone/fax: (612) 935 4910

Whales
in the
Classroom

T-Shirts!

NOW AVAILABLE

IN FULL COLOR!

Whales *in the* Classroom

Style shown: WBT101